The Magic Presence™

THE "I AM" DISCOURSES

"I AM" RELIGIOUS ACTIVITY
OF
SAINT GERMAIN FOUNDATION

The "I AM" Religious Activity represents the Original, Permanent, and Highest Source of the Ascended Masters' Instruction on the Great Laws of Life, as first offered to the Western World by the Ascended Master Saint Germain through His Accredited Messengers, Mr. and Mrs. Guy W. Ballard.

In the early 1930's, the Ballards established Saint Germain Foundation and Saint Germain Press, which under Saint Germain's Guidance have expanded into worldwide organizations that offer to mankind the True Ascended Master Teachings on the Great Cosmic Words, "I AM"! Saint Germain Foundation strives to keep this "I AM" Ascended Master Instruction in Its pure, unadulterated form, free from any human interpretation, personal monetary gain, or proselytizing, as It is a Gift from the Great Ascended Masters and Cosmic Beings to bring Illumination and Perfection to mankind.

Hundreds of "I AM" Sanctuaries and "I AM" Temples exist throughout the world, where the Teachings are applied in "I AM" Decree Groups. The Books of the Saint Germain Series are available through the Saint Germain Press and in many libraries and bookstores. For further information, please contact:

Saint Germain Foundation
Saint Germain Press, Inc.
1120 Stonehedge Drive
Schaumburg, Illinois 60194

(708) 882-7400   (800) 662-2800

THE "I AM" DISCOURSES

BY THE
SEVEN MIGHTY ELOHIM

THROUGH
LOTUS RAY KING

SAINT GERMAIN PRESS, INC.

Editors' Note

The Inner Light and Feeling have been held as of first importance in presenting this
Truth; and the words used to express that Light and Feeling are those which are most
direct and easiest to comprehend by the reader. There have been a few minor correc-
tions in this text for clarification; therefore, the printed text may differ slightly from the
original tape recording.

Trademarks and Service Marks of Saint Germain Foundation include the following:
The Ascended Masters Instruction on the "Beloved Mighty I AM Presence,"* The
Ascended Masters' Instruction,^{SM} "Beloved Mighty I AM Presence,"* Daughters of
Light,* Heart of Heaven,^{SM} Honor Cross,* Honor Cross Design,* "I AM",* "I AM"
Activity,* "I AM" Angels of Light,* "I AM" Ascended Master Youth,^{SM} "I AM"
Ascended Master Youth Newsletter,* "I AM" COME!* "I AM" Emblem,* I AM" Music
of the Spheres,* "I AM" Reading Room,* "I AM" Religious Activity,* "I AM" Relig-
ious Broadcast,* "I AM" Sanctuary, * "I AM" School,* "I AM" Student Body,*
"I AM" Study Groups,* "I AM" Temple,* "I AM" Violet Flame,™ The Magic Pres-
ence,™ "Mighty I AM Presence,"^{SM} Minute Men of Saint Germain,* Music of the
Spheres,* Saint Germain,* Saint Germain's Pantry,^{SM} Saint Germain Foundation,* Saint
Germain Press, Inc.,* Shasta Springs,* Unfed Flame Design,* Violet Consuming
Flame,* Violet Flame,* *"Voice of the I AM"* *

Library of Congress Cataloging-in-Publication Data
The "I AM" discourses / by the seven mighty Elohim through Lotus Ray King. -- 1st ed.
    p. cm. -- (The Saint Germain series ; v. 14)
    Includes index.
    ISBN 1-878891-61-8
    1. I AM Religious Activity.   I. King, Lotus Ray, 1886-1971.
II. Seven mighty Elohim.   III. Series.
BP605.I1815   1995
299' . 93 -- dc20   95-9289
                                                                        CIP

CONTENTS

Elohim of Peace

Elohim of Purity

Elohim Hercules

Elohim Orion

DEDICATION

HIS SERIES of Books is dedicated in deepest Eternal Love and Gratitude to our Beloved Ascended Masters Saint Germain, Jesus, Godfre, Lotus, Nada, the Great Divine Director, the Great Host of Ascended Masters and Cosmic Beings, and especially the Seven Mighty Elohim.

These Dictations were given through our Beloved Accredited Messenger, Mrs. G. W. Ballard, whose pen name is Lotus Ray King. They were recorded during Saint Germain Foundation Classes of the "I AM" Religious Activity in various parts of the United States of America from 1950 to 1970, and appear in print here for the first time.

May the reader be raised a Spiral Higher when studying these Mighty Words of Instruction and absorbing the Ascended Ones' Radiation, which is an essential part of every Ascended Master Discourse.

TRIBUTE

T IS with very great Love, Joy, and Gratitude that we offer a Tribute from our Hearts to the Group of Great Cosmic Beings known as the Seven Mighty Elohim. In the Bible They are titled the Seven Builders around the Throne. We bow before Their tremendous Power which built this System of Worlds.

To have the privilege of Their Visits, Instruction, and Understanding of the Sacred Fire is the Greatest Joy that can come to anyone in this physical world, outside of each one's Ascension. To acknowledge Their Sevenfold Flame—that iridescent Flame of all the colors—in the forehead, is the first step in receiving Their Cosmic Gifts.

The Cosmic Being known to us as the Great Divine Director said: "The Seven Mighty Elohim are Authority over everything in this World; even I come under Their Direction! They are greater than I, and I am obedient to Their slightest Direction. When these Cosmic Builders of the whole System of Worlds come and offer you the use of Their

Sevenfold Flame in Its Violet Flame Power and Victory of Cosmic Christ Action, then My Dear Ones, you should understand it is because of the crisis of the hour in outer conditions which has made that necessary. You as individuals would not be given that just for your own individual growth or expansion of your Light for your Freedom. *These Powers only come into the outer use of mankind because of the need of the mass of the people of the Nation and the World.* But as you are offered this, if you render the Service, then great will be the Authority and Power and Action of the Violet Consuming Flame of the Seven Mighty Elohim within yourselves, and then you will find Illumination coming from within you; and you will automatically understand many things which have been difficult for you to comprehend up to this time." *("Voice of the I AM," March 1975)*

"I AM" THE COSMIC SEVENFOLD FLAME!

"I AM" the Cosmic Sevenfold Flame
    Of Sacred Fire all Supreme,
Its Blazing Colors pouring forth!
    Their Cosmic Power from God's Great Stream
Are Life and Light and Beauty rare,
    All Freedom and God's Loving Grace,
In Cosmic Victory everywhere–
    For God's Great Love must light each face!

"I AM" the Cosmic Sevenfold Flame
    Of every Quality of God,
All God's Perfection must rule man,
    And bless the Earth where man hath trod.
From God hath come Life's Greatest Gifts,
    And all that blesses rules above;
For "I AM" is the Self that lifts,
    And ever pours out all God's Love.

"I AM" the Cosmic Sevenfold Flame
    That manifests throughout our Land!
It floods forth all Its Cosmic Fire,
    The Healing Peace from God's own Hand!

Within Its Glory and Its Heart
    Forever dwells God's Greatest Power,
And every Life Stream is a part
    Of that Great Life which flows each hour.

"I AM" the Cosmic Sevenfold Flame
    From Realms of Cosmic Love on High.
It is God's manifesting Self,
    And helps all as they hurry by!
From Its Great Blessings all may draw,
    And none will ever find It gone;
It is God's Treasure-house of Life,
    It flows and flows forever on.

"I AM" the Cosmic Sevenfold Flame!
    Its full Authority does reign,
For none can ever stop Its Fire!
    Lo! It through Love dissolves all pain!
It is God's Music and God's Health,
    And in that Flame are all made Pure.
So, to It give your love, your all;
    For it is God's own Heart secure!

"I AM" the Cosmic Sevenfold Flame,
    Whose Mighty Presence all behold,
And know whence come God's Blessings rare,
    Through It all secrets must unfold.

In Glory and in Vict'ry True
    That Mighty Flame has ever won,
And so It shall forever bless,
    Until each Life becomes a Sun!

Oh, the Glorious Cosmic Sevenfold Flame,
    That Marvels blaze and all inspire,
Become God's Mantle to all here,
    Forever raising them all higher;
Make all remember God–"I AM"!
    Illumine them by all Its Light,
And show them all God's Word can do!
    Come! Blaze Thyself in all God's Might!

Lo! Mighty Cosmic Sevenfold Flame!
    Make all on Earth a Cosmic Sun,
And ever hold within Thy Heart,
    Our lov'd ones here till Vict'ry's won!
Then by Thy Great Commanding Voice,
    Thy Clarion Call speak to each ear,
God's Great Command– "I AM" God's Flame!
    "I AM" Your Freedom! Your way is clear!

                                        Chanera

(Reprinted from "*Voice of the I AM,*" June 1945)

THE "I AM" DISCOURSES
By the Beloved Seven Mighty Elohim

──────────── ✳ ────────────

CHAPTER I
Beloved Elohim Arcturus

Santa Fe, New Mexico
November 30, 1957

Beloved Ones of the Sacred Fire, I trust I may leave with you tonight a Power that I want you to use, and I know you will be happy to use as soon as you see the results It produces in your world.

You who know of Us, and you who know the Seven Mighty Elohim, should give daily recognition to the Sevenfold Flame of the Seven Mighty Elohim in your foreheads, because That is the Focus of the Faculties of the Sacred Fire within you, within the intellect, in the mental body. While your Beloved Higher Mental Body projects Its Powers and those Faculties through the outer self, We, in the Projection of that Sevenfold Flame through the brain structure,

1

are the Cosmic Sacred Fire Guard of your mental processes if you will but give Us recognition.

The mass of mankind knows absolutely nothing of where the Powers of the intellect come from, what they can do to protect those Powers, or how to use Them only constructively. The Sevenfold Flame of the Seven Mighty Elohim is placed in the brain structure of every human being to be the Guard of the Faculties of the Higher Mental Body that the individual must have and use in outer physical conditions, if you are to attain Mastery.

Mastery means the constructively qualified energy and eternal control of all energy and all substance, wherever you move anywhere in interstellar space. That's what the Ascended Master or Cosmic Being is!

You begin to manifest that control by your conscious awareness of the Sevenfold Flame of the Seven Mighty Elohim within the brain structure enfolding the entire activity of your mentality. Mankind is in the condition it's in because it does not recognize or give conscious attention to Our Sacred Fire within the brain structure, that would always protect against misuse of the powers of the mind if individuals would only give Us recognition.

Those of you who understand your "Beloved I AM Presence" by your awareness of Our Sevenfold Flame within the brain structure, you may have tremendous Power, both mentally and physically, come into your outer use as you understand This, as you love It, and as you demand Its Cosmic Protection of everything in your Life Stream to control all your experiences.

Now, those of you who are doing creative work, regardless of the channel, must use the Creative Powers of the mind. If you would always *call forth the Creative Powers of the Seven Mighty Elohim and the Victory of Their Sacred Fire Use,* you would find much less delay in your accomplishment; and Inspiration that you might need from time to time would almost come flooding over you. It would come so rapidly and offer Itself into your outer use.

You could not possibly give recognition to Us and *call for Our Sacred Fire Inspiration and Perfecting Control of everything you do in the outer world,* without having It manifest! You could not ask your "Mighty I AM Presence" and Us to charge That into you and into your affairs without having the Answer! It's just as certain to manifest through you and to you, as that you make the Call. When you call for Our Sacred Fire Inspiration, My Dear Ones, there is not a thing that the Mind of God contains that you couldn't have!

The Mind of God, the "Beloved I AM Presence," the Great Central Sun, and the Sacred Fire

Source of all manifestation is ready to flood in and around you Its Boundless Blessings, Its Miracle Powers, Its Inspiration without limit, and Its Manifestations that have never yet come into outer existence anywhere.

That is why the Beloved Saint Germain in the beginning of this "I AM" Instruction said to you, if you would acknowledge *"I AM" the Great Creative Heart of God,"* marvelous ideas would come to you and you would bring forth things that have never been brought forth before, because the Great Creative Mind of God is the Sacred Fire. It contains the Limitless Ideas of Eternity and is ever revealing more of Its Perfection into outer manifestation.

If you will draw This into your outer conditions—always with the awareness that whatever you produce is only Perfection, and that Perfection reveals the Love and the Glory and the Powers of God to glorify the Source that gives Them to you—My Dear Ones, you would make progress so rapidly, the Blessings that would flood your world would be indescribable, and you would go forward a century ahead of the rest of mankind!

When you *demand that everything in your being and world be compelled to be constructive, be compelled to be Invincible against evil, be compelled to produce Perfection that makes all Life happy, glorifies the Universe, and bears witness*

to the Master Presence of your "Beloved I AM" and to the
"I AM Presence" in the Great Central Sun—when that is
your constant thought, that is your constant Picture
within, that is your constant Devotion to Life, every
action you would perform in the outer life would
produce Perfection for you, would lift you above the
turmoil of the outer world, would give you such Supply as you do not even believe exists, and you
couldn't lack for a single thing! How could you?

   We are the Seven Builders of Creation, and as
the Seven Builders We have Unlimited Supply with
which to build, and We build only Perfection that
brings Happiness and Freedom and Glory to all. We
build only what is constructive! But My Dear Ones,
mankind down here, bound as it is in its own discordant creation, is constantly reabsorbing the destructive pictures it has created in the past, which are
manifesting now in the present as outer world conditions, and if you do not cut yourselves free from that,
you would go on indefinitely in the cycle, drawing
that back into yourselves and producing more limitation outside.

   The hour comes when you must either completely and unconditionally take your Stand that you
won't have anything in your world but the Perfection
of God—and when you have decided that with all you
are or have, you will remember to give Us recogni-

tion. You will remember you have a Sevenfold Flame of the Seven Mighty Elohim within your forehead. You will remember that the Sacred Fire contains all Perfect Thoughts, all Perfect Pictures, all Perfect Manifestations, and Revealment of the Divine Plan for you and all you contact!

If you want the future revealed, it comes from within the Sacred Fire, not from within the outer world pictures or conditions that suggest themselves to mankind. So I am taking you deep tonight into the Heart of Freedom, if you want to come, and there "I AM"! *(applause)* Thank you so much, Precious Ones.

If you want to come, there "I AM" within; for I assure you the Flame of the Sacred Fire which is My Special Quality and Service and Responsibility to Life, abides within your brain structure. Therefore, I can reach you at any moment to give you the Blessings that will fill your world with Perfection forever. Thank you so much; and won't you be seated, please.

I am pleading with you tonight because it is you who must take your Stand that everything in your being and world shall manifest Perfection, to glorify your "Mighty I AM Presence" and the Ascended Host who are your Protectors. All mankind put together cannot protect you, Dear Ones!

Your Protection has to come from the Sacred Fire of your "Beloved I AM Presence" or Us. Therefore, whatever Guard you have of anything constructive must still be an Action of the Sacred Fire. When you see how much mankind has used the Faculties of the mind that are loaned to it by the Higher Mental Body, and how they have used those Faculties to create only destruction, I think they need Us!

They need to know something about the Sevenfold Flame of the Seven Mighty Elohim within the brain structure that can guard the mind against misuse. It can guard the feeling against discord. It can guard the world of the individual against destruction, and It is the Sacred Fire Authority of Perfect Creation!

So Blessed Ones, if you take your Stand and *demand that destructive pictures shall not come into your being or world,* if you take your Stand to prevent that, then We can give you very much greater Assistance. You can have very much greater Supply. You can have automatic Protection, and Inspiration without limit could flood your world from day to day, till you would be the marvels of the age and the rest of mankind would wonder how you do it!

Now if you want to be mysterious, of course that's one way to do it; but that's not always desirable.

If I were you, I would go ahead and get the
Momentum built of Perfection in your own world.
Don't forget this: whatever you command or desire
to have manifested in your outer experience or in
your world, do not fail, before you try to do it, to *call
forth Invincible Sacred Fire Protection, Ascended Master Protection that can never change; and draw your Protection before
you try to create anything!* Then a destructive force does
not come in and either delay you or distort what you
are trying to do, or destroy something after you've
built it!

Here mankind has lived age after age after age,
one Golden Age after another. The Great Presence of
Life has just flooded Perfection in every Golden Age,
and yet mankind has destroyed its own handiwork!
You do not need to go through that experience
longer.

With this Knowledge of the "Mighty I AM
Presence" and your conscious use of the Violet Consuming Flame, if you will take your Stand to *demand
the manifestation of the Pictures of Perfection in your world,
everything*—you issue the command and *call the Sevenfold
Flame of the Seven Mighty Elohim to stand your guard before
the Perfection manifests, and hold everything you do sustained
and protected, to bring happiness to Life and glorify your
"Mighty I AM Presence."* If you will start with that, you
will not know what failure is. You will not know de-

lay. You will not know lack of any kind, and you cannot produce anything but Perfection!

Now, I think you have experienced imperfection long enough. Your trial and error method is accepted in the outer world as the only way you can find things out in this Universe, and to Me it's pitiful! God Beings, with the Flame of God in the Heart, the Flame of the Seven Mighty Elohim in the forehead, endowed with the Authority of Command, given the Use of the Great Creative Word "I AM", Beings of Free Will, Beings of the Creative Power of the Sacred Fire in the Life Stream—and they go on, century after century and age after age, because they prefer to look to the without instead of to the within.

I am shattering tonight some of the old racial habits under which you have functioned for many lives. As the Mighty Saint Germain told you, people century after century stay in distress and problems and limitation because they are content to stay in limitation, because it takes Strength, Power, and Determination to arouse the outer self to shatter the limitation. If mankind does not exert that Strength, then it stays in the limitation!

I am cutting away, as much as the Cosmic Law will permit, your acceptance in the past or your willingness to stay in limitation. If you arouse yourselves and are determined to be Free, you shall be Free! *(applause)* Thank you so much, Precious Ones.

Now, you cannot stay in limitation if you will remember to call forth the Authority and Power of Victory of the Unfed Flame in the Heart, and the Sevenfold Flame in the forehead, and the Heart Flame of your "Beloved I AM Presence" which you call forth first!

There is no human being alive who will call to that Beloved Heart Flame of the "Mighty I AM Presence," the Heart Flame of the outer self, and the Sevenfold Flame of the Seven Mighty Elohim into all outer physical conditions, you cannot stay in limitation if you *ask that Sacred Fire to fill everything in your being and world with the Perfection of the Divine Plan fulfilled, and you call forth the Ascended Masters' Invincible Protection of all Perfection you desire manifest!* Then whatever you do that is constructive is held sustained and ever expanding!

You know everyone likes to be fashionable. My Dear Ones, let us start a new fashion, one this world never heard of: that in the midst of the chaos of the outer world a group of you enter into this use of the Sacred Fire, and make your own individual beings and worlds the Perfection of the Seven Mighty Elohim of Creation, Invincibly Protected and forever expanding Its Love and Happiness and Blessing to Life. And live *your* way.

If I were you, I would set It into action, but fail not to *call forth the Sacred Fire's Invincible Cosmic Protection before you begin.* Then, as you produce manifestation, you will not have interference from those who are jealous. You will not have obstruction from the selfishness of the unawakened of mankind. You will not have delay because of lack of understanding, and you cannot have failure. I think that's worth working for! *(applause)* Thank you so much, Precious Ones.

Now, with these two things that have been given you recently—*the Demand to your "Mighty I AM Presence" and the Ascended Host to show you the Truth of your needs in Blazing White Light, so you cannot misunderstand; then your calling forth to Us for the Sacred Fire's building of Perfection in your world, after you have called forth Its Invincible Cosmic Protection*—you may go forward to very rapid accomplishment and very Great Victory. I cannot stress too much the warning that was given you the other night, when you were told to *keep demanding, always, that your "Beloved I AM Presence" and the Ascended Host show you in Blazing White Light the Truth you need to know, the information you need to have, to do what is necessary for your own protection, your own supply, and your sustaining of that which is constructive!*

Now, please do not fail in this, because the individual who will stand steady with that Command, will never be interfered with by psychic forces again the rest of Eternity. If you knew what the psychic forces have done to Life, to drive individuals to the second death, you would reach up and take this like you take your next breath. I am here to arouse you tonight to the necessity of this, because unless you shut out psychic forces, because of their hypnotic control of the masses of the people, they seek to interfere with anybody and everybody that wants to do anything constructive.

Those psychic forces pretend to be the Christ. And there is nothing of the Christ in the psychic realm! I shall say that with your Beloved Saint Germain for Eternity! I shall shock mankind awake! Otherwise they will be enslaved for only God knows how long.

There is nothing good in the psychic world! So Beloved Ones, tonight, I come to protect you, if you will listen to Me! *(applause)* Thank you so much.

Those psychic forces have made mankind fail lifetime after lifetime after lifetime, and yet individuals will not stop playing with it! Psychic forces can touch your feeling and you not even know that they are anchored within you for six months. But when they've got you under their control, you have this failure and that failure and something else, and you don't know why you don't succeed after all your efforts.

If I were you, I would arouse myself, and I would *demand every Power of the Sacred Fire in this Universe blast me free and my world free from everything psychic; and for the rest of Eternity keep me untouched! (applause)* Thank you so much.

Now, do you remember what your Beloved Saint Germain said to you about the psychic realm? He said, "That is the main activity and sustaining energy of what We call the sinister force of the World. That is the accumulation of the energy of the anti-Christ." Now, is there anything there you want?

Don't let people fool you and tell you other things. We know! Unascended mankind does not! So long as people fool with the psychic forces, they'll never attain the Ascension.

That is the main realm of the accumulated energy of all mankind's emotional world, wherein is the filth of existence, wherein is the crime and the insane destruction of war.

Therefore, I come to bring you the Protection of the Sacred Fire, if you will use It. I plead, and I shall continue to plead until you are awakened so completely to the Power of That which I offer, that you never fail to use It! As you go forward to any constructive accomplishment, you call for its Sacred Fire

Cosmic Protection before you begin; you call for the
Seven Mighty Elohim's Sacred Fire Victory and
Power of Its Perfection. You call for your "Beloved
I AM Presence'" Divine Plan fulfilled, with that
which you have the capacity to do, and to keep yourselves untouched by anything psychic, ever again in
all Eternity!

If you will do this, you will go forward in leaps
and bounds! You won't know what interference is!
You won't know what lack is of any kind, and you
will have Friends that you will never have until you
do this!

So the Seven Mighty Elohim of Creation have
many Powers and Gifts to give you, and They are
awaiting every opportunity. They offer without
money and without price; and you cannot have any
result from the Gifts They give except Perfection for
Eternity, and Happiness you have sought so long and
have not yet attained!

The Powers of Life are Infinite! The Love of
Life none yet understands. The Door to Victory
stands wide open before you if you refuse to look any
longer upon that which is destructive, or allow it to
impose its imperfection upon you or your world!

You either must stand completely unconditionally in the World of Perfection, or you don't! You
can't serve two masters and make any progress

ahead. With this Knowledge of a Call to the Unfed
Flame in the Heart of your "Mighty I AM Presence,"
the Call to the Unfed Flame in your Heart, the Call
to the Sevenfold Flame of the Seven Mighty Elohim
for Our Assistance to produce Perfection in your
world, you cannot possibly fail! You couldn't fail to
be answered!

So from tonight, I hope you will feel Our Determination to assist you, Our Determination to protect you; and if you will give just this little Obedience
that is required, it is so little compared to the Gift that
We can give. We do not want to see you struggle
longer, when, with arousing Determination to have
the Sacred Fire fill your world with Its Perfection of
Eternity, Invincible against human creation, you may
set yourselves Free on the Pathway of Perfection, and
know no limitation. You know only the Happiness of
Victorious Accomplishment; and the Power that it is
your privilege to use brings to you and to all, Blessings without limit for Eternity!

So go forward, and know My Sacred Fire ever
stands by your side to enfold you, and produces Perfection and Protection, as you give It Recognition.
Call It into outer action! Use It in all you do, and refuse to let the pictures of the outer world's imperfection and chaos come in and ruin you and your world.

In the Sacred Fire is the Boundless Supply you all crave. It's what you call for. It's what you must have with which to do the Will of God; and there is no lack in the Sacred Fire's Source of Creation.

My Dear Ones, begin to use This! Call forth your Protection! Call forth your Supply! Pour your love to your "I AM Presence," and *demand everything in your being and world be compelled to yield you the Perfection of the Sacred Fire, Invincible and Victorious over all in this World forever!* Every Being of the Sacred Fire will come to your Assistance, stand by your side, and fulfill your Call beyond your fondest dreams! This Freedom I want you to have, because you need It to assist your Beloved Saint Germain.

So if you will come with Me, you know no longer the strain and struggle and distress of human experience.

Let us go forward and help you to be Free as soon as possible, as you enter into the Joyous Use and Invincible Demand for your Perfection by the Sacred Fire that knows no failure and no end!

May you be enfolded in the Sun Presence of Its Powerhouse and make everything in your world Its Perfection, till like a Mighty Sun you are a Magnet to draw all you contact up into that Perfection also! We shall ever be with you in Cosmic Power! Thank you with all My Heart.   (*Record CD 954*)

Excerpts on the Sevenfold Flame

Beloved Arcturus

My Service to the mankind of this World is the blending of the Unfed Flame in the Heart with the Sevenfold Flame in the forehead. I wish to show you tonight, whenever there seems to be uncertainty in the mind or confusion as to what is the right thing to do, how to release the right Direction you want to receive.

Still the feeling for a moment, and hold the Picture of the Unfed Flame in the Heart expanding up through the Sevenfold Flame of the Seven Mighty Elohim in the forehead. Then, see It arising into and being enfolded by the "Mighty I AM Presence." . . .

The purpose of the blending of the Unfed Flame in the Heart and the Sevenfold Flame of the Seven Mighty Elohim in the forehead, is to bring you to the point where the Sacred Fire takes Its Dominion within the outer self, and gives the Higher Mental Body Its Unconditional Control of outer physical conditions.

This is not only in the flesh structure of the body. It radiates forth as a Sun Presence and enters into the atmosphere around you, enters into everything in your world, so the great Law of Ever-expanding Perfection of the Sacred Fire's Love goes on giving of Itself. It keeps pouring forth through the individual the greater Perfection from the Ascended Masters' Octave, until the outer self becomes the Master Presence of the Violet Consuming Flame's Control of all outer manifestation.

(Violet Flame Series I)

Beloved Arcturus

The Sevenfold Flame of the Seven Mighty Elohim means in the outer consciousness that the same Mighty Power of the Heart Flame from the Great Central Sun and the Physical Sun are together anchored within the Life of the outer self, that Its Expanding Perfection and Eternal Purifying Love and Illumination may forever make the outer self a Sun Presence of Our Love and the Great Central Sun's Outpouring of Ever-expanding Glory and Perfection and Mastery over all manifestation, no matter where you go in interstellar space—because wherever you pass in outer activities of life, the only Authority over all manifestation is the Great Central Sun's Sacred Fire Heart Flame. And the Sevenfold Flame of the Seven Mighty Elohim is the concentration of that—in the outer use of every individual embodied—into the substance of this World.   *(Record CD 1600)*

CHAPTER II
Beloved Elohim Arcturus

Shasta Springs, California
August 15, 1953

Beloved Ones of My Heart, let us enter in tonight to the understanding of what is within the Heart
of Life, your Heart, the Heart of the Physical Sun and
the Heart of the Great Central Sun, and the Heart of
every Focus of Life that is the Individualized Flame
from the "Mighty I AM Presence" in the Great Central Sun; for I want you to enter deep into the use of
this Magnificent Power that abides in each of you and
is constantly offering Itself to you for your Freedom.

In contacting the conditions of the outer world
in the daily problems which you solve, or in the activity you choose to express, before you try to do that
which is in outer manifestation, enter into the Heart
Flame of your own "Mighty I AM Presence," first of
all through your love to that "Presence," and then to
whatever Ascended Master or Cosmic Being is concerned with the activity you choose to express. And
when you wish to understand something that is of the
greater Perfection in the Higher Spheres of Life, as

you call to the Heart of your "Mighty I AM Presence" and the Heart of an Ascended Being, fail not to ask that your "Mighty I AM Presence" show you all you need to know at this time concerning what you wish to do, but show it to you in the Light within the Heart of your Ascended Master Friend to whom you call.

As you ask for information from the greater Spheres of Activity, try to go directly to the Heart Center of the Source that gives you the information of Perfection. And then, when you need to know something and you say: "*Show me what I need to know from within the Heart Flame and the Light of,*" for instance, "*the Heart of our Ascended Master Saint Germain,*" there will come back to you clearly and without interruption that which your "Mighty I AM Presence" wishes to use through you at that time. For as It releases and accomplishes certain greater Activities to fulfill Its own Divine Plan through you, It calls to one or more of the Ascended Host for Assistance while It is releasing the greater Power into your outer use. And it is the Assistance which the Ascended Master or Cosmic Being is giving, that you need to understand in the outer in order to cooperate most perfectly with your own "I AM Presence" in fulfilling Its Desires in the physical world that produce magnificent Manifestation and Perfection everywhere you choose to call It forth.

It wouldn't make any difference how much of this world's goods you were required to use, if your "Presence" chose to accomplish some magnificent thing in the outer, It is the Authority for the use of everything in manifestation. Therefore, when you ask It to show you what you need to know within the Light in the Heart Flame of the Assisting Master, then the enfolding Radiance of that Master's Love will show you the Light, and give you unmistakably the Direction by which you can let the greater Mastery of your "Presence" reveal Itself through you in outer action. Then you become Perfection expressed, because with the Radiation of an Ascended Being, and your "Presence" releasing Its Direction through you, there is no such thing as an obstruction or delay.

You may have anything you want without limit, so long as you understand this and cooperate with it. And to some degree, Beloved Ones, It is a revealing activity of your "Mighty I AM Presence" similar to the Cosmic Screen upon which the Blessed Saint Germain revealed to the Children in the Cave of Symbols that which He wished to do through them, and which He wished them to hold their attention upon until He accomplished their Freedom for them.

So it is with you when you understand that within the Heart Flame of your own "I AM Presence" is the Eternal Divine Pattern and Direction and Plan for you, every instant the rest of Eternity, and that within the Light from the Heart Flame of an Assisting Master is the Love and the conscious enfolding Radiance to assist your own "I AM Presence" to release Perfection. Then, as you are aware of what is to be accomplished, the outer self could not make a mistake ever again. Seeing the Divine Perfection from within and feeling the enfolding Protection from the Assisting Master, the outer self could not be disturbed and would not fail once to cooperate in every way, that these greater Powers might act through the outer self at all times in Perfect Divine Order.

Then, My Dear Ones, when that becomes a habit within you, there will be no longer mistakes or limitations or the struggle you have experienced in the past. This can become the Cosmic Screen for you, upon which Life places the revealment of Its own Magnificent Glory and Its unmistakable Direction to you.

And the easiest way to feel This at first, until you come to the point where you see It, is to command the stillness at the solar plexus and relax, not with a sense of drowsiness but a sense of balanced ease and peace within the feeling world. In that, there is no tension in the nerves and when the nerves are relaxed, the Light from the "Presence" is flowing through the body without interruption. And in that Light which comes into the body through that Ray from the Heart of the "Presence," in that Light are the Pictures and is the Power or Pressure you require to bring to the outer self anything that will fulfill the Divine Plan. And in the enfolding Radiance from the Love of the Assisting Master, there comes the Atmosphere and Light Substance from Our Octave that is your insulation against the discord of the outer world that would interrupt what your "Presence" was trying to accomplish.

Now, in this you will have tremendous Assistance so far as your health is concerned. When you hold the Picture of the Light Substance from within that Ray of Light entering into the brain structure, spreading Its Light through the nerves, going into the spine and sending Its Light through the nerves again, then sending It to every Point of Light in every cell of your body—then as that Light comes in and expands Its Pressure, so to speak, through the flesh structure, the Assisting Master pours the Light of His or Her Love around you, fills your atmosphere with It, you breathe It in, It unites with the Light from your "Presence," and the human creation in between must subside and be consumed.

If you will just set to work with joyous determination to hold these Pictures of Perfection within your thought, and then love them with your feeling, seeing and demanding that They be revealed to you in the Light from the Heart of your "Mighty I AM Presence," you will find such Glory, such Power, such Security, such Accuracy coming into your outer activity as will bring you Joy for Eternity. And in trying to accomplish this, if I were you, I would *demand the Ascended Masters' Concentration and Use of all the energy and substance of the outer self held forever within the Illumining Love that must produce Perfection.*

When you understand this Magnificent Power of the Sacred Fire as that Love which illumines everything by Its own Perfection, then you will not just feel that the Love to which We refer is some transcendent Activity in Our World, and unattainable by you until you come into Our Octave—because that is not the condition of Life! Everything that is in Our Octave We stand ready to flood into your outer use, because the greater Perfection of Life is always giving of Its greater Blessing to that which is lesser. And the greater Perfection is a Magnet that draws the lesser into the greater. Therefore, that is the Law of your own existence. It is the Law of all Life—that everything must become greater and more perfect, as you enter into the Great Cosmic Release of those Activities of the Sacred Fire that are commanded by Love alone.

There is no part of Life in the unascended state that can interfere with the Fire of Our Love! I want you to feel that; I want you to be enfolded in It. And if you hold the Picture of My Heart's Flame enfolding you in My Love, as surely as you hold that Picture will My Love enfold and hold you in the Perfection of My Octave. And since it is part of My Great Service to Life to consume the veils between the Flame in the Heart and the Flame in the head, then as you enter into the use of the Light of My Love, you will find those veils becoming thinner, the resistance less; the delay will cease, and all of a sudden with the great Ease and Power of Freedom, you will throw aside your limitations as if they had never been. Now this is what takes place, My Dear Ones, in the Fulfillment of the Great Divine Plan of Our Assistance to Life.

As the Mighty Victory told you—and imagine what must take place from the Higher Octaves when such a Miracle occurs in the physical—when He said to you: "I have taken a man in the gutter and in one wave of My Hand consumed that creation and raised that individual back into the Glory and the Victory of the Light of Freedom." It is that Power which We want you to use while yet unascended. You do not have to be completely Ascended in order to have the use of these Great Powers of Life that set your fellowman free. All you need to be free from the human is the Light and the Love of the Divine. And the Love from your "Presence" is an actual Substance of Light. It isn't just a feeling or just a wave of vibration.

The Radiation of the Love from the Heart of your "I AM Presence" or from Us is an actual release of the Electronic Substance of Eternal Light. It is the Radiation or the tiny sparks, as it were, that are poured forth from the Great Flame of your own Individualized Focus of Life, which is the Eternal You from the Great Central Sun. And therefore, when We speak to you of the Light of Our Love, or the Love of the Sacred Fire or the Powers of that Sacred Fire, try to realize those are just as real and tangible as any physical thing you have in this room tonight.

Don't struggle longer, Precious Ones. Don't fight through the outer world conditions, trying to find a little fragment of knowledge here, and a little fragment there, and a little assistance here, and a little assistance there, when in unconditional turning of your attention to your "Presence" when you want to know something, with love and the feeling of that love intensely from your Heart reaching up to enfold your "Presence," you *ask It to tell you the Truth of what you want to know in the Light of Its own Heart's Flame, and make you know It unconditionally in the outer,* you would not have to ask but a few times till your "Presence" would set you free from the limitations of centuries.

That is what We have been driving at when We reminded the Student Body again and again to be through with the struggle of human problems. And you can't be through with the shadows unless you have the Light, and you cannot have the Light unless you have the Sacred Fire from whence It proceeds. That Sacred Fire is the Eternal Life of the "Mighty I AM Presence" in the Central Sun. The Radiation of the Light is the Gift of Its Love and the Substance out of which the manifested world of form ever gives you of Itself.

So when you train the intellect to hold the Picture of Dazzling White Light before you, and still the feeling until your "Presence" shows you the Truth you want to know, it will not take long. You do not have to sit down for hours in order to accomplish this. You ask for It, you keep the energy in the feeling world quiet and relaxed and at ease; and in the midst of something, with which as a rule you are not at all connected with what you want to know—in the midst of something else, when you least expect it, will come the full Flash of the Answer to your Call. And as soon as you keep the Door open continuously, it will answer you then instantly and show you the Picture at the same time.

Now, I set up a Guard for you, if you will accept it, so you will not become entangled with any of the pictures of the psychic stratum or the things of the physical world that do not produce Perfection for you. Just because you see a picture in the mind of some thought or a form or something does not mean that that is necessarily from your "Presence."

We long ago set up the Guard for the "I AM" Student Body by asking them always to make the Call: *In the Name of the "Mighty I AM Presence," in the Name of the Ascended Jesus Christ, show me your Light!* And demand that whatever your "Presence" gives you, It gives you in the Blazing White Light of Its own Heart's Love; and then nothing in the world can fool you, no psychic force can drive in, no lie can approach, and no psychic substance can intrude into that which is your Sacred Domain of connection with your "Almighty I AM Presence" or the Ascended Host. Then there will be no veils between; you will see as clearly upon the Blazing Light of the Love from your "Mighty I AM Presence'" own Heart that which you wish to know, as plainly as you can see the lights in this room tonight—plainer!

If you choose to use the term: *Show me the Truth I demand to know upon the Cosmic Screen of the Light of Eternal Love!* —and see for yourselves whether the Floodgates open, and that uncertainty of the past will

forever be removed from your world. You can positively live in the World of Blazing Light Substance
which is the Love from the Heart of your "Mighty
I AM Presence." You can have that same Blazing
Love from Our Octave, and you may have that as
your Powerhouse, your Illumining Presence, that
never permits a mistake, that never permits anything
human to be recorded upon the Eternal Screen of
Life.

The Great Miracle of Eternal Light ever stands
before you ready to reveal to you anything in the
Universe, so long as your attention goes *first* to your
"Beloved I AM Presence," and you ask that the Heart
Flame of your "Presence" blaze the Light of Its Love
to you and tell you the Truth you want to know.
God is not so difficult to understand. The Truth of
the Universe is not so far away that you cannot reach
It. You do not have to go through long centuries of
struggle and strain and endurance of suffering in order to find God, in order to reach the greater Perfection of Life, in order to reach up into Our Octave and
know That which is greater than yourselves.

My Dear Ones, remove from your consciousness tonight, remove from your mental and feeling
world every concept of the past that you have to go
through long periods of suffering in order to attain
the Perfection of the Ascended Host! That thing has

been, from a standpoint of outer world suggestion to mankind, imposed upon all the people of this World for centuries in so-called channels that ought to tell the people the Truth.

The Great God Presence of Life, the "Mighty I AM" in the Central Sun, the Great Presence of Love Supreme, the Great Presence of all Perfection and Boundless Power does not need suffering to teach you where the Perfection of Life is. You cannot make that which is Perfect dependent upon evil; that is unthinkable! And therefore, no longer accept the nonsense of human hypnotic suggestion.

Take this which I give you tonight, and in all the feeling of love at your command to your "Presence" first, ask It to tell you the Truth upon the Cosmic Screen of Its Eternal Light in the Heart Flame of Its Love and show you the Truth you need to know, show you the way to stop trouble, show you how to annihilate the limitations and mistakes of the past, show you what your "Presence" wants you to have in the future, show you the Love from the Ascended Masters' Octave, show you the Health and the Strength that belongs to you. And then with love and gratitude in your Heart, reach up and accept It and know It is yours; bless your "I AM Presence," bless every experience through which you have passed, but hold onto nothing that is of discord.

I am determined that these suggestions to mankind through the centuries under the guise of various channels of the outer world must roll back as a scroll from Life and release Life in unascended mankind to the realization of what the Love of God means to the Universe. How can a God of Love want you to experience the discord of human viciousness in order to find the Light? It is absurd! It is a complete reversal of what ought to be. If you want to know the Truth of any situation, demand It upon the Cosmic Screen of Eternal Light from the Heart Flame of your own "Presence'" Love, and see for yourselves the Scepter of Power you may use.

You are not subject to the limitations of the race consciousness of mankind through the centuries. Suppose there has been an accumulation. Someone must forgive it. Someone must consume it. Someone must replace it by Perfection. And after all, what are limitations? As the Mighty Victory said, in one wave of His Hand, He could annihilate those limitations of God-knows-how-long standing.

If you believe what the Messenger decrees every night—for the Fiery Truth of the Victorious "Mighty I AM Presence" to go forth and annihilate every lie that has ever been told, annihilate the hypnotic control of the people, annihilate mankind's mental confusion, annihilate human desire which is nothing but

human selfishness and human creation—if you understand what is in that Decree and you will make this
Call to the Heart Flame of your own "Mighty I AM
Presence'" Eternal Love, Love *cannot* refuse you.
Love *will not* refuse you. Love will give you more
than you dream exists, and Love will set you free
from every limitation. It doesn't make any difference
who, when, where, or what built it; if it touches your
world, you can be free when you take the Authority
of your own Life Stream and demand the Truth of
that Perfection which is God's Divine Plan for you.

Oh, so many Blessed Ones with such marvelous
ability, marvelous accomplishments, marvelous Powers stored within the Causal Body waiting for centuries to bless you in the outer, go on for years or life-
times not knowing what to do and yet wanting to do
something that they feel they ought to do. And if
they saw It, they would know Its Magnificence and
feel the Victory of Accomplishment.

Many times people say, "Well I don't know
what to do. I wish I could find my right place." And
they just go on in that uncertainty—while if that same
energy, in one intense determined Call were sent to
the "Mighty I AM Presence" with intense love, and
*demand to be shown the Truth in the Blazing Light of Eternal
Love, and demand your way to Freedom by the Love of*

Eternal Life, you would have to have the Answer to your Call.

You could call to your own "I AM Presence" or you can call to Us. We are *One* with that "Presence"; and if you were tonight to ask Me to show you the Truth in the Eternal Light of the Love of My Heart concerning any problem, concerning your Nation, concerning the assistance you want to give, I would be obligated under the Cosmic Law to tell you the Truth of what you want to know. So there is no such thing as failure for the individual who demands the Truth of Life revealed in the Light of Eternal Love, by the Sacred Fire and Authority of the Great Command.

I am determined to break down your limitations, to strip you of your problems and your struggle, annihilate the memory of your mistakes, and clear the pathway ahead of you, that I may blend the Flame in the Heart and the head and make you a Being of Light strong enough to go forward and render the service to your Nation and the World, which forever closes the door to any more of this human thing that so dishonors God's Universe.

Contemplate frequently, until you get the feeling within, that your "Beloved I AM Presence" and the Ascended Host are Beings of Love so great that They are not interested in anything but every opportunity to expand Its Blessings of Love and Light and the Sacred Fire throughout the Universe to bring everlasting Happiness everywhere. Your "I AM Presence" isn't interested in your mistakes; if It were, It would have them in Its own World, and that is impossible, which is a good thing.

Oh, Beloved Ones, come tonight into that Eternal Light of Our Love, demand what you will of Eternal Truth, and see whether We give It to you or not. You have had volumes of Instruction from Our Octave in these Magnificent Dictations over the years. And why do you suppose We have flooded you with this? That you may render the Service to the Nation that must come, and the Nation render the Service to the World that must come! And it must come by the Power of the Sacred Fire. It must come by the Eternal Truth in the Eternal Light of the Universe, the Miracle Light of Eternity in which no lie can exist. And therefore, you step upon your Pathway of Light with absolute certainty of your knowledge, your power, and the way and means by which you attain your goal.

Then, My Dear Ones, you become a Beacon Light, like a Sun, and the Magnetic Power of that Sun will draw everything into the same Perfection where Love alone pours Its Light everywhere to bring happiness and ever create the Universe about you and fill it with the Glory of Its Almighty Command.

Oh, My Dear Ones, let Me blend these two Flames. Again and again and again return your attention to your "Presence," until there is not one bit of obstruction between and you can go forth in the attainment of the success that should long ago have filled your Nation and the World. Demand this same revealment to the people of the Nation. *Demand that the people of this Land be compelled to know the Eternal Truth in the Miracle Light and the Sacred Fire of that Love that sustains the Universe. Demand that the people be compelled to know the Truth that abides only within the Eternal Light,* and then fire them awake with that Truth, until Its Blazing Presence has consumed the hordes of the shadows.

Whatever you want to know, you can know so long as you demand the Truth revealed to you from within the Cosmic Light of the Love and Sacred Fire of your own "Mighty I AM Presence." And you keep insisting that that "Mighty I AM Presence" tell you the Truth about this! *Tell you the Truth about this! Tell you the Truth about this in the Eternal Miracle Light of Love Supreme;* and see for yourselves that which clears away the limitations and the mistakes and the problems of the past. This will allow you to balance your world.   And when your world is in balance, then there comes forth from your "Presence" the Fulfillment of every Desire of your Heart, so long as it be constructive.

Every constructive desire is God's Desire for you. But when you demand to know the Divine Plan's Fulfillment in the use of those constructive desires, then it should be revealed to you; and the moment you ask, there is the Power in the Universe to answer. And that way you can go forward; you live in God's Universe then, and the race consciousness of mankind can never touch you again. And this I give you as a Promise and as a Revealment of the Great Blessings of the Cosmic Law.

Once your "I AM Presence" says to Me: "Blend the Flame in the Heart, the throat and the head of this My Instrument"—once I blend those three Flames into One, never again can you be touched by limitation or mistakes or problems. That day, you are through with the shadows of human creation. And I assure you, it is the most joyous Freedom. It is like stepping out into the sunshine after you have been in a dungeon of darkness; you step into a Freedom that you see always within the Light. And then as your attention is held upon that Light, you become aware of the Light in others, and you deal with the Light of Life. And that which seems to be the human accumulation around it is no more than a cocoon; you break it

apart, throw it away or consume it, and you let loose
the butterfly from within. And the Soul arises on the
Wing of Its Eternal Love, and It lives in the Universe
of Light, eternally Free. You are that, My Dear Ones.
The Flame within your Heart is bound by the race
limitations and mistakes of the past, but the Hand of
your "Presence" and your Heart's Call can snap
every limitation that has ever dared to try to limit you
in your onward progress to Freedom.

So let us go forward, and with no uncertainty
take the Hand of your "Mighty I AM Presence." Use
the Power of the Great Command, and *demand the
Eternal Truth of the Miracle Light of the Universe reveal to
you anything and everything you want to know or need to
know to release Perfection everywhere, to raise all you contact,
to move forward with the Fullness of your Freedom and stand
forth the Fulfillment of your Victorious "Mighty I AM Presence'" Divine Desire for you.* This is the Divine Plan of
Life; and as you call This forth, it would be impossible for Us not to answer you. *Your Victory is as certain
as your Call.*

So, Precious Ones, you will begin to understand
now why We have asked you to live within the
World of Our own Hearts' Flame, to know what the
Fiery Love of Our Hearts' Flame means to Life, to
know what the Victorious Cosmic Christ can give to
you, for It is this Eternal Light of Everlasting Love—

until you go forward, and never again are you to be bound.

Then, My Dear Ones, delay no longer! The hour is here! The World needs you. Your Freedom can come by your own attention raised to the Heart Flame of your "Mighty I AM Presence," with the Demand that Its Light fill your world and tell you the Truth and the Law you need to know to hold the Mastery of conditions here, until Freedom once again fills the Earth, and Peace claims all into the Octave of Light for Eternity.

I tell you frankly, when That occurs, you could not have ill health, you cannot have financial lack, you cannot have limitation or struggle, you cannot make mistakes; you become Invincible to the human creation of this World. And then you move on a Pathway that ever grows brighter and brighter until you enter into Our Octave, and it is as natural as breathing. There is nothing mystical, there is nothing hypnotic, there is nothing limiting, there is nothing hidden about it; it is just the great natural, Wonderful Way that Life has provided for you to have Its greatest Blessings, Its boundless Freedom, Its everlasting Victory over that which has been but the passing shadows of mankind's desires that did not want to obey the Love of the "Presence."

So let us go forward; and remember, My Dear Ones, as each one of the Seven Mighty Elohim comes forth to give you the Victory and the Power of the Heart Flame and those Qualities which each of Us gives to the Earth, as you enter into the use of each one's Special Qualities through that Love, you become the balanced, directing, creative Activity wherever you abide. And then you know what is in Our Hearts. We know what is in your Hearts, and your Hearts will take you forward safely to your final Victory.

It is so wonderful, when mankind for so long has been in the stress of the shadows, to see the daylight approaching wherein consciously, clearly, of your own Free Will, you can take the Hand of your "Presence," release Its Light, know Its Truth and command Its Love to do all things, until your service in this World has raised it also into the Perfection of Our Octave. I await your Call, and I shall be so grateful to render this Service, and I shall forever enjoy your Freedom with you.

May My Heart's Love and the Light of My Life tell you the Truth, fill your world, reveal all that belongs to you, and help you manifest it to the outer world until all want only the Light and the Freedom which It forever bestows.

Thank you with all My Heart, and the Love of My Heart's Flame shall light your way unto your Ascension. Thank you.

(Record RU 119)

CHAPTER III
Beloved Elohim Cassiopeia

Chicago, Illinois
January 5, 1964

Beloved Ones of Our Hearts, today I bring you the Cosmic Illumination of Our Love. And I trust as We anchor It within the brain structure of each of you, with your permission, We want to enfold you in the clear Comprehension and the Wisdom from the Ascended Masters' Octave and especially That of the Seven Mighty Elohim of Creation, that you may have the use of It in your outer activities more naturally, flowing constantly, and ever present to help you as quickly as possible do that which needs to be done in the outer and *know* what needs to be done.

Very often you make the Call to your "Beloved I AM Presence" or to some Ascended Being to show you the right thing to do in some condition that you need to handle. That's quite all right, but very often when you have been shown, you do not do that which has been shown to you.

Today I am anchoring into the mental and feeling world of each of you the Power of Our Sacred

Fire's Illumining Presence of Purifying Love and Our clear Comprehension, not only in the intellect, but We are anchoring This within your feeling world— and It is enveloped in the Heart Flame of each of the Seven Mighty Elohim to hold Protection about Our Feeling in you, which means the Strength of the Sacred Fire in you to hold control of your feeling, so you at all times have Our Protection and Strength to do the right thing.

You might know intellectually the right thing to do, and you might feel you are capable of doing it, but Our Heart Flames' Love within and around you is Our Awareness and Our Feeling of the Power to do it. Now there is more to it than just that: You might have the full Conscious Knowledge of the right thing to do. We can fill you with Our Hearts' Flame of Our Feeling of the Strength and the Power to do it; but if you do even what you know is the right thing to do at the wrong time, it will not fulfill the Divine Plan.

So there is a moment that is the right moment to do a thing, in order to create Perfection, sustain It, and let It become Master over the surrounding conditions in which you move. So when We offer you Our Cosmic Illumination and Our Hearts' Feeling of the right thing for you to do, there will always come within you not only the feeling of your ability to do it, but there will come a control of the energy in the outer self that will show you the *right moment* to do it and the *right way* in which to do it, because you might do the *right thing*, but if you do it at the wrong time it will not produce Perfection. If you delay it, then the very Protection you need would not and could not manifest.

So Our Wisdom is the Illumination of the mind, the Strength of Our Sacred Fire Love in your feeling. But Our Life, Our Life's Control of Manifestation will pour Its Sacred Fire Presence in and around you and enfold you in the Power to accomplish what you need to, and will be the Force that controls you to enable you to do the right thing at the right time and hold the balanced control of physical conditions, so that the Perfection of your "Beloved I AM Presence" can come through you into outer physical conditions and be surrounded by Our Protecting Sacred Fire, so what you build manifests Perfection for you and manifests Perfection for the Life surrounding what you build. And that is a tremendous Cosmic Action and Cosmic Power of the Radiation from the Ascended Masters' Octave.

When We speak of Radiation to unascended beings, It is always the Release of Our Ascended Master Feeling of Our Hearts' Control of any manifestation, whether it be in the mind, in the feeling, or in the physical conditions of this World.

These three things are imperative in order for you to hold the balanced control of the Forces you are using and must use to create Perfection in this world that manifests the Divine Plan fulfilled and yet, keeps that Perfection from being touched by the desecration or the selfishness and the downright destruction of the forces in the world around you.

Many wonderful things have come forth, Beloved Ones, of magnificent Perfection which mankind has created in every civilization; and then that Perfection has been dissolved and consumed or desecrated or misused by those who would not do right at that time.

This which We are calling your attention to today and which We are giving into your Life Stream, is Our Ability, Our Power to do the right thing at the right moment, that sometimes you need in an instant in order to be the Protection of yourselves and others, that makes you Invincible against the discordant forces in the outer world.

So in this way the Power, the Ability, the Sacred Fire, the Illumination, and Our Love of Our Life Streams is always, then, anchored in and around you, and in an instant that Flame can flash. That's the Sevenfold Flame in the forehead; and as It flashes and enfolds the physical body, It fills you with the feeling of your ability to do it; and it is enough control of your outer self to enable you to do it perfectly and at the perfect moment.

This is the Cooperation of the Inner and outer. This is the Balance of Love, Wisdom, and Power. This is the Cosmic Illumination of the Seven Mighty Elohim of Creation, who are the Builders of everything in the physical world that you call the Powers of Nature or Forces of the Elements, or the construction of a Planet.

There is always this Threefold Activity. And now that We have called It to your attention, We can stimulate, as it were, the Action of the Sacred Fire of the Seven Mighty Elohim within you, and It will expand in and around you and clothe you in Our Feeling. It will expand in and around you and bring Illumination to the mind, show you the Picture, show you the Way and Means of doing that which produces Perfection. But It is more than that! It is the actual control of your outer self, so that at a moment you can do *the right thing, in the right way, for the right purpose,* that holds sometimes Protection, sometimes Victory that must come at an exact moment.

So when it is necessary sometimes for you to have Protection, or you to give Protection quickly to someone else, there must be within you Our Flame,

Our Life, Our Illumining Consciousness, Our Feeling, and Our Control of Manifestation. Then when there is the need in the outer world—either yourselves or others—your "Beloved I AM Presence" has Our Enfolding Life; and then as the need comes up, when the outer self starts in to render that assistance, or just quietly create something that is magnificent, there is Our Heart Flame in you to be the Sacred Fire's Control of your physical bodies, as well as your mental and feeling world.

So you have perfect cooperation from the mind, the feeling, and the outer physical muscular structure of the body.

You have the Perfect Cooperation of your "Beloved I AM Presence," Its Divine Plan revealed, Its Heart Life expanding through you the Wisdom and the Design It wishes to manifest. And you have Our Enfolding Sun Presence of Our Cosmic Light Substance enfolding you in your ability to do what needs to be done, and therefore We can give you Our Ability! Now this is a tremendous thing from the Inner Standpoint, as well as from the outer.

You have seen, and I am sure have had experiences many times, when a person that sometimes has had no training at all is suddenly able to do some astounding things. Well that is why, because when the outer self has not had the training and has not learned to do what is necessary to produce certain manifestations, We who are that Consciousness and that Life in the Ascended Masters' Octave of Immortal Perfection can extend Our Heart Flame, Our Life, Our Love, Our Feeling, Our Pictures of Perfection in and around you and hold That about you steady, until your "Beloved I AM Presence" comes through and controls the condition that manifests Perfection for you. And Dear Hearts, if the mass of mankind would only understand This, and not dash into a thing without preparation, your trial and error method would be wholly unnecessary.

You can just as well know the Full Perfection of what needs to be done before you start into it, as you can after you've tried to build something, and then it isn't adequate or doesn't fulfill the Divine Plan and you have to start all over and do it again.

This is the Prevention of the mistakes that you have made in the past. It is the Prevention of the limitations under which you've struggled; and more than that, when you really become accustomed to using This, This is the Prevention of your problems. So It is a very necessary, practical way of Life by which We can assist you! (applause) Thank you so much. Won't you be seated please, and just remain so!

Now many times the "Presence" shows you the right thing to do, but you do not always know the

Perfect Way to do it, or the most necessary way to do it; but when We enfold you in Our Life from the Ascended Masters' Octave, It is the Life that has been used to create this World and the Magnificent Perfection that has been here many times. And It is Our Life's Experience of using these Master Powers of Life to design Perfection, to make you feel Perfection, to enable you to desire Perfection, and to clothe you in the most wonderful, efficient way of producing that Perfection.

One reason I am bringing This to your attention today is because someday when you begin to use the Powers of Precipitation or Etherealization, you will need to make this Call so that what you have precipitated into your hands will be the Perfect Thing you desire, and not something that has come through the outer self and is distorted and therefore would disappoint you.

This is the Balanced Use of the faculties of your Life, your mind, the Power in your feeling and your Powers of Creation. The Power of Design and the Power in the feeling is the energy in your Life which you give to it.

You must give your Life to whatever you are going to design and create; and therefore Our Life, enfolding you in Our Hearts' Flame, is the complete Ascended Master Balanced Control that controls you so you do the right thing in the right way and the most wonderful Harmony and Perfection that enables your "Beloved I AM Presence" to reveal to you and give to you the Perfection It wants to bring through you. And Our Perfection that We have used for centuries can come in and around you and be a Power to assist you because It can only produce Perfection for you. Therefore Our Life, Our Sacred Fire Love which We give to you for this Service would always know and be the Self Control to do the right thing at the right moment. Therefore, in all Creative Activities you need the Enfolding Heart Flame of the Seven Mighty Elohim of Creation to enable your own Life Stream to come through you and hold the Control around you while It fulfills Its own Divine Plan through you!

That is why there is a Flame of each of the Seven Mighty Elohim in the brain structure of the physical body. That's not placed there by accident. It's placed there because It is Our Ascended Master Life Flame that has been through this World, is Master over it—I mean through not this particular World, but I mean a physical embodiment wherein the Master Powers of Life were unfolded and used to create Magnificent Manifestation. And Those are the Powers We have used when We created a World or a System of Worlds.

Therefore, that Life is the Almighty Perfection of the Sacred Fire that always creates Perfection and which cannot be used by imperfection. Therefore, there is no such thing as distortion or failure or desecration of any kind. When Our Flame enfolds you, It controls everything in Perfect Balanced Action; and if mankind would only learn to use This and cooperate with Us, all the miscreation due to experimentation would be wholly unnecessary.

From now on, whenever you have a responsibility or something that you need to do in your service to Life, or your creation of something in the physical world, *call for the "Beloved I AM Presence" and the Ascended Masters' full Ascended Master Illumination of the God Way to do this,* so no matter what you have to do, don't dash into a thing with just the human desire that you know how to do it.

Yes, you might have done a similar thing many times, but there is a God Way, a Good Way, a Harmonious Way, an Invincible Way, a Perfect Way to bring things into manifestation without strain or struggle, and you may know ahead what you are going to require to produce the Perfection you want to create, and then use it only for the Fulfillment of the Divine Plan.

This takes out of your feeling world all human desire and lets the Eternal Divine Desire in your

Heart, the Eternal Desire of the Sacred Fire from the Seven Mighty Elohim of Creation, the Eternal Divine Desire from your "Mighty I AM Presence" and Higher Mental Body come in as one Activity of the Sacred Fire. And then when It flows out here to control physical conditions, It cannot help but produce Perfection for you. This takes the work out of your daily activities.

We have long, long reminded you to use the word "activity" instead of "work," because "work" to the outer self contains within it a sense of struggle or exhaustion or effort. But I assure you, Beloved Ones, when the Sacred Fire creates something, there is no effort in it that is any kind of discord or strain or struggle.

You have no idea how This will help your health, because you will not work under the tension of outer world conditions to which you have been accustomed.

Now, the habit of doing things the outer physical way is of long standing, both in yourselves and in the race consciousness of all mankind; but Our Sacred Fire Power of Creation is of long standing too, much longer than your human creation. So you can have Our Momentum!

I want you to feel how We can fill you with Our Life's Sacred Fire that has already created Magnificent Perfection for aeons of time. If you study music for instance, or electronics, or anything with someone who is an expert in that line, you listen and you do exactly what you are told, and obey the law of whatever you are studying. One day, you are able to do everything that the one instructing you has been able to do. That one can confer upon you, or explain to you and within you the right way and means of producing that same thing, and you can produce what your instructor has produced.

Well, there is no difference, Beloved Ones, between that and Our Ascended Master Octave. The Life We give you, the Love We give you, the Energy We give you from Our Ascended Master Octave is the Life, the Energy, and the Love and the Feeling that We have used through aeons of time to always produce Perfection.

If you will use This, We are giving you the Security of Life. If you will do This, We are giving you the Security of Perfection, and there isn't all mankind put together can override or overrule or destroy or desecrate Our Sacred Fire Power.

So if you want the Perfection from Our Ascended Master Octave, *you have the Open Door through the Sevenfold Flame of the Seven Mighty Elohim in your own forehead.* That's the channel through which We must give It. That Sacred Fire controls the brain structure.

Its Radiation controls the emotional body, and Its Enfolding Love can control your muscles, your nerves, everything you do with the physical body, so what It does, It does in Perfect Cooperation with your "Mighty I AM Presence," with your outer physical structure, and with the Ascended Masters' Octave.

I am trying to teach you today the Divine Way to live Life, the Original Way by which you created Manifestation in the two first Golden Ages. So I am not giving you something you have not already used in times past. This is not new. I am simply reminding you of That which you knew once, which you used in the two first Golden Ages; and It always produced the Harmony and the Beauty and the Perfection which existed and in which you dwelt during those centuries of your embodiment.

So now, as We go forward to the Creation of more Magnificent Perfection in the civilization that must come within this Nation, We want to be of very great assistance to every one of you individually, if you will begin to use This which We offer.

I hope We may be of very practical assistance to you. I hope We may be your Partners, and who knows, maybe We will be the Contractors of the future! *(applause)* Thank you so much.

Now, if This were applied in the government of your Nation, in the control of your business, in the management of your affairs, your homes, or your association with the rest of mankind, Beloved Ones, It's the Harmonious Way by which you can get the cooperation of those individuals who will be concerned with that which you are doing and will cooperate with you, give you their best, and control the whole situation harmoniously.

This is the way by which mankind can live together, accomplish the Fulfillment of the Divine Plan, and dwell harmoniously in the physical octave. Do you not think it is needed this hour as you look at the world's activities? If you don't, We do!

When you see the discord in mankind's feeling, surely you must realize there is some God Way to live Life that does not have to go through that constant destructive element of discord and impurity and downright desecration of the use of Life and the substance and energy of this World.

We are giving you the Eternal, Harmonious, Divine Way to live Life, to correct conditions here, to build the Perfection of the future, and to use the Magnificent Blessings the Powers of Nature have provided here, or that We can lower from the Ascended Masters' Octave and bring into your use for the Service of your fellowman, yourselves, and the producing of That which will raise everybody into the Purity and the Harmony that does bring about the Ascension.

Everything We give you will converge to the accomplishment of your Destiny in the attainment of the Ascension. And in your assistance to your fellowman, as the mass of mankind become aware of the Ascension, you will assist the Earth itself to its Purification and Self-Luminosity till it, too, becomes Ascended as a Sun.

So We give you a very practical way to live Life; and when you do not know what's the right thing to do in physical conditions, don't look to the outer through individuals who are not harmonious. If you are going to get information, seek the harmonious channel, but *ask for the Seven Mighty Elohim's God Way to do what needs to be done to fulfill the Divine Plan at the right moment in the right way, but whatever you do, make it Invincible against any human creation.* Then everything you create will bless everybody and everything you contact, and you will close the door to the discordant experiences that have, many times, so disappointed you and so limited you that you have almost given up your effort to do that which you have the capacity to do.

Now when you start to do something in the physical octave, stop a moment and *ask your "Beloved I AM Presence" to flood you with the Great Central Sun's*

Cosmic Illumination, and the Ascended Masters' Sacred Fire Illumination that knows the Ascended Masters' Way to create what you want to create, and then, be at Peace!

Make your Call and hold the Harmony; and as you hold steady within that and you *ask Our Hearts' Flame to enfold your physical body, blaze through everything in your feeling world, and fill your mind with the Cosmic Illumination of the Seven Mighty Elohim of Creation, and into the outer bring the Ascended Masters' God Way of doing everything,* We can fill you with That which comes from Our Octave. Then your "Beloved I AM Presence" can fill you with that which It wishes to give you, and you can go forward and correct conditions in the physical world by the Sacred Fire from Our Realm of Life—because all conditions in this World that need purifying and correcting, if they are going to be corrected permanently, must be filled with the Ascended Masters' Sacred Fire Presence and Heart Flame in order to hold the Purity, the Harmony, the Balance, and the Possession and Control of the Energy and the Intelligence necessary to produce that Perfection and protect It. Then It can expand to bless you and bless everybody you contact, and you will not struggle!

You have decreed to prevent all mistakes, limitations, problems, and struggle! Every bit of that can be prevented by the Ascended Masters' Sacred Fire

Presence and Way of doing everything, and We can teach you many, many, many Ways to do things that mankind has never yet used.

You can be the Advance Guard of the Incoming Civilization, and you can just as well know the Harmonious Way to do many of these things that seem so complicated and are complicated, that cause confusion. And you can *call to the "Beloved Mighty I AM Presence" and the Ascended Host to show you the Sacred Fire's Way of Manifestation;* and if you care to call, We are more than happy to enfold you in Our Illumining Mind, Our Illumining Consciousness, Our Illumining Harmonized Feeling, Our Illumining Sacred Fire Presence and Control of everything in your outer self.

So you can have the *Magic Way* to live Life and let your "Beloved I AM Presence," the *Magic* Presence of all Eternity, come into you and show you what a Magnificent Way Life has used throughout the aeons of time to sustain this World, to ever expand the Perfection that's been brought here, if mankind would just stop the creation of discord.

If you will use This, you will find Our Enfolding Sacred Fire Love will not only prevent discord in you and your world; but wherever you abide, It will hold helpless the discord in the world around you through which, sometimes, you have to pass.

So Beloved Ones, if you care to accept Our Sacred Fire, practical Way to live Life and use the God Powers of the Sacred Fire to control conditions in you and around you, We are the Givers of those God Powers, those God Flames of Manifestation, those God Ideas of Illumination to the mind. We are the Givers of the God Feeling of Life which Our Love is, and We are the Givers of the Way and Means of controlling your physical bodies and the conditions around you, that never create discord; and I think it's time some unascended beings learn how to live that Way! *(applause)* Thank you so much.

Now one more thing! Whenever you wish to start out on something that's a new project or some responsibility you have to carry, even just solving your problems sometimes mentally, if you simply stop everything of the outer and *call to your "Beloved I AM Presence" to come in, and then call to the Seven Mighty Elohim of Creation to fill you with and enfold you in Our World of the Master Control of the Sacred Fire's Perfection and the Sacred Fire's Master Way, the Elohim Master Way to produce the creation you desire, or the control of the condition you desire*–then you open the way for Us to fill not only you, but the conditions around you with the Sacred Fire of Our Hearts' Love. And whenever That comes in, We prepare the way so that when you come in and have anything to do there, automatically your "Presence" has control of the outer self because it is Harmonious; the outer self is quiet.

If We enfold you in Our Hearts' Flame, I'll assure you, you can't get the flutters and nobody around you can disturb you. You could stand in the midst of turmoil and you'd be as calm as the Great Great Silence; and that's Mastery. That's the Power you need in order to hold the Harmony within by which your own "Beloved I AM Presence" can pour into the situation whatever Sacred Fire produces Perfection for you. And We—the Enfolding *Cosmic* Sacred Fire of Our Life blazes in and around you That which raises you and everything in this World into the same Great Perfection which Our Love has produced in Life. So from this hour, you can use Our Sacred Fire Love to do positively anything and everything you have to do in the physical octave, if you care to make this Call to your "Presence" and to Us, and We shall await your Call.

We are waiting to give you experiences that will delight you beyond description. We are willing to give you the Sacred Fire Love which Our Mastery is, that you may use It to master conditions here. And if you and We can't master conditions here, it won't be Our fault. We'll teach you how, and you do not have to become slaves of circumstance or allow yourselves to be imposed upon by the conditions of the people in this outer world that will not, as yet, live the Harmonious Perfect Way of Life.

We are the Giver of the Gifts of Life. We are the Seven Builders of Creation, and I assure you, We have not forgotten how to build Perfection. So if you want Our Perfection and the Secret of how It's done, how It's created in this World, the information is yours. There is no Secret from Our Side. We give the Limitless, but you must open the Door.

So when you want It, call for It! When We give It, you accept It! When you accept It, go ahead and use It, and your world shall become the Perfection of Our World, and your world will bless the rest of this World, just the same as Our World is ready to bless you!

I hope you can and will remember to experiment with the Use of Our Sacred Fire God Way of Life to do everything and give Us the opportunity to flood your beings and worlds with Blessings that, as yet, mankind has never used in this World. And We are ready to open the Door today! So I trust you will come with Us! *(applause)* Thank you so much, Precious Ones.

Now, We offer you the Enfolding Miracle Mantle of the Seven Mighty Elohim of Creation's Mighty Love to Life; and Our Perfection from the Ascended Masters' Octave can come in and around you, bless you, enfold you, protect you, and control you, and take you forward to the Victory for which you've called, and a Victory that you can give to every part of Life wherever you abide, because you can teach others to call for This, as We are teaching you.

So from this hour remember, We are the New Way to live Life—new so far as this modern generation is concerned, but We are the Original Divine Way of God's Creation. And now We want your world to be Our World and God's Way of Manifestation so everything that you contact will be a Blessing to you, a Blessing to the World, and you will not have time to be discordant!

We can shut the door, today, against the world of discord. As you set This into action, form the habit of using Our Elohim Sacred Fire Hearts' Control of everything ahead of time, and let Us show you the way out of the discord in the outer world; and wherever you abide, you will be like the Sun Presence, the Sun Way to live Life that illumines all things ahead of you, and you stand enfolded in Our World and are able to give to the rest of Life that which We give to you.

So the Heart Flame of Our Love ever goes on and renders Its Service, till mankind turns its back on the shadows of human experience, and once again lives from the Heart Center and does that which only produces Perfection and Freedom and the Victory of the Ascension for all, and It can only come by the use of the Heart Flame of the Sacred Fire's Love to Manifestation everywhere forever.

So We want to draw you into that Realm, Our Heart Realm of the Right Way to live Life, and you shall have all the Blessings We can bestow! Thank you with all My Heart!

(Record CD 1002)

Excerpts on the Elohim Music of the Spheres

Beloved Cassiopeia

When mankind desires Me, I will be there in Manifestation! When you who know this Law, and whom We have loved because of your Calls to Us and your *Song of Adoration* to Us—We have heard your Calls. We have felt your love. We have come closer and closer, and will continue as long as you want Us. But I say to all of you, I challenge you to spend twelve to sixteen years, eight hours a day, like you have to go to school, calling to Me for the Cosmic Wisdom of the Universe, and see what your world will contain.   *("Voice of the I AM," January 1980)*

Beloved Cyclopea, Elohim of Music

Thank you, Beloved Ones, for your Calls and your Adoration as it went forth this day through the Song to the Seven Mighty Elohim.

You would be utterly amazed if you could see how far the Light went, how far It expanded, and what We will do through that; for It shall come back to you infinitely for Eternity to bless you because of the Call in the lyrics of that Song. That Call goes to the Heart of Creation and the Music shall sound for

Eternity, and it shall bring Purity and Illumination, and it shall bring Our Response to the Hearts of those who have called.

So, thank you for your Adoration in that Song; and thank you for your Life's energy that went forth on it. I assure you Our Life and Its Flame of Love shall go on and on and on, until It purifies, illumines, and raises all into Our Perfection for Eternity.

(Cassette SGC 27, side 2)

Beloved Sanat Kumara

In your Song of the *Seven Mighty Elohim*, sometimes when your love becomes very great and those Great Beings choose to qualify that with Their Healing Cosmic Love, They stand in a circle around the building. And as your Life's energy goes up in that Musical Form, They suddenly flash, each one, His Sevenfold Pink Flame into and around that, just as if They covered It with Their Hearts' Flame. And then It begins to arise and expand and expand; and as They work with It, pouring into It anything else which is required, It is a thing of Beauty to behold. This is what We want you to see, Beloved Ones. One day these things will be visible in the atmosphere of Earth—I trust not too far distant.

("Voice of the I AM," November 1976)

Beloved Goddess of Music

Can you imagine the Power that We could release or that the Seven Mighty Elohim could release if you had a building where, for twenty-four hours without cessation, five to ten thousand people at one time were to sing the Adoration to the Seven Mighty Elohim—sing for an hour, then another group take it up for an hour; and keep that going for just one twenty-four hours! Can you conceive of what We could do with that much of your Life's energy? Well, I can! I am trying to give you My Feeling and Concept. There is not any condition on this Earth that you could not change when that is continued!

("Voice of the I AM," March 1944)

Seven Mighty Elohim
by Lotus Ray King
From the Music Dedication by Lotus Ray King, 1943

This Song, both music and lyrics, is a direct Answer to our intense Call that through Music we may all constantly pour to Them our love, adoration, and gratitude for Their Immeasurable and Eternal Gifts of Freedom and Illumination, and for being the Open Door through which Their Help comes to us instantly and without limit. May all who sing, play, or hear this Song feel the Mighty Reality of these Great Beings, Their Enfolding Presence and Love pouring out constantly and bringing Eternal Freedom in "the Light of God that never fails"!

* * * * * *

Note: Since 1988 a Musical Adoration to the Seven Mighty Elohim is conducted on the last weekend of the "I AM" Senior Conclave, held annually at Shasta Springs, California. The program lasts twenty-six hours and the Song is performed continuously, approximately one hundred times. The performance consists of shifts of "I AM" Students singing the Song, and joined successively by the Conclave Choir and Orchestra, organ, piano, handbells, harps, and instrumental ensembles.

CHAPTER IV
Beloved Elohim Cassiopeia

Chicago, Illinois
January 5, 1966

Beloved of My Heart, I trust tonight We may be of Service to you and bring again into your Life Streams a Strengthening Power of the Cosmic Light and Intensifying Activities of the Sacred Fire that will enable you to feel your Mastery over conditions in this world more quickly.

Before you start anything, and many times in the day when you just have an instant where you do not have to keep your attention on something in the outer that you are doing, *train the outer intellectual consciousness to turn your attention many times a day, for just a moment, to your "Beloved I AM Presence," and ask It to fill you with Its own Heart's Flame, and what It knows you need to know from moment to moment to exert your mastery over conditions of the outer world.*

When you call to Us to fill you with what We know you must have in order to exert your Mastery over any wrong conditions, do not fail to keep calling forth Our Elohim Fiery Christ Blue-Lightning

Illumining Truth, Illumining Wisdom, Illumining Power, and Illumining Victory and Strength of the Light within yourselves!

Keep calling forth Our Elohim Fiery Christ Strength of the Light in you that makes you strong enough to do that which We know you are going to have to do in the outer, either to render your service or hold protection.

When you fill yourselves with the Seven Mighty Elohim's Fiery Christ Strength of the Light, and the Illumining Truth, the Illumining Consciousness that We know you are going to need to master any condition in the outer that is wrong, and to make you victorious over the wrong in the outer world, then We can flood in and around you in a moment, if you have made this Call—just like We dropped a Sun Presence around you, and the Intensifying Love of Our Hearts' Flame fills and surrounds you within That, a more Intensifying Presence of the Golden Flame.

This brings Illumination to the brain structure. It brings the Illumining Consciousness of the Seven Mighty Elohim into the control of your attention, and to hold the balance, the reason in full control of your emotional world, your feeling world, so you do not take on or swing into the pressure of the discordant feeling of other people.

Now, as you go forward from day to day in your service to the outer world, try to train yourselves not to dash into a thing till you have had just a moment, just an instant, of turning your attention to your "Beloved I AM Presence," and *the Call to Us to fill you with Our Elohim Strength of the Light that makes you Our Victory over evil out here!* Then We can charge into the mind Ideas in a moment, that you might need to use the next moment in outer world conditions in order to hold protection around yourselves, or to enable constructive activity to be brought forth in the midst, sometimes, of chaos.

Keep charging yourselves with your "Beloved Mighty I AM Presence'" and the Seven Mighty Elohim's Fiery Christ Wisdom, Fiery Christ Truth, Fiery Christ Illumination, and the Fiery Christ Knowledge of the Seven Mighty Elohim, Knowledge that We have, and which We can give you and show you how to overcome conditions in the outer world that otherwise you feel perfectly helpless before.

Now, this has a powerful Protecting Activity within your emotional body, because if you have made this Call and then you hold still just a moment, We can pour Our Sacred Fire within you; and while It flows within you, We can also pour It around you to govern conditions in a moment that you do not know the next moment might occur.

Now, this has a Protective Power for your automobiles, anywhere you travel, and in any condition in which you associate with other people who, sometimes, act quite quickly or impulsively in outer world activities.

Charge yourselves with Our Seven Mighty Elohim Fiery Christ Wisdom and Fiery Christ All-Knowing Mind that knows ahead of time what We know you are going to experience—because We see into the outer. We know the forces that are acting. We know what they intend, and We know how vicious they are, when sometimes you don't; and then, Beloved Ones, *fill yourselves with the Ascended Masters' Fiery Christ Mind that will not let you deceive yourself!*

Many times people think they are doing something from one motive, and another motive in the feeling is acting completely to get its own way. This is why I bring this to your attention tonight. We see these things. We know what is acting. We know what is in the atmosphere of Earth. We know many things that it is well if you do not know them. This will make you master over circumstance.

It is well worth every effort you will make to take the time to *call to your "Beloved I AM Presence" and to Us to fill you with Our Illumining Wisdom, and Our Fiery Christ Alertness that brings Illumination ahead of time as to what you are going to need in any situation to prevent what is wrong, and give that which is constructive an opportunity to hold the Victory of what is right!*

This is a Powerful Activity of the Wisdom of your own "Mighty I AM Presence" and the Ascended Host; and *this is why there is the Sevenfold Flame of the Seven Mighty Elohim within your brain structure,* because there must come a continual pouring from the Ascended Masters' Octave into your own mind of the greater Perfection, and the greater Mental Activities of the Universe that design more and more Perfection to come into the physical world to fulfill the Divine Plan.

Mankind left alone, Dear Hearts, in this World, without this greater Illumination from the Seven Mighty Elohim of Creation and the Cosmic Beings and the Ascended Host—how much do you think the intellect of man, left alone, would accomplish?

There is not enough Light in the brain structure of unascended beings to be the strength of the Light to make them do that which is constructive without the Assistance, the Protection, the Amplification, and the Enfolding, Illumining Presence of the Seven Mighty Elohim of Creation, is the reason We have given you Our Life to start on, and Our Enfolding Sun Presence of Our Hearts' Flame, that knows for aeons of time ahead what is to be done. We can give you as much of this from day to day, or from Call to

Call that you make, that enables you to understand conditions in the outer world around you; and to avoid the things that the destructive forces want to impose upon you, because you do not understand how vicious and destructive they are, or who they are, or who they are working through at any moment.

So, the Illumination which We ask you to call forth into yourselves, is that you may be illumined enough ahead of time to hold your protection; and you are going to have to have It, that's all! When the masses of mankind are lying so continuously in channels of the outer world, if you do not have Our Fiery Christ Truth, how are you going to know what's the right thing to do to protect yourselves?

This will not only clear your consciousness, but this will draw around you the Fiery Christ Truth of Our Life, of Our Power, of Our Light and Illumination that will help others that come near you to know the Truth also. And through Our Radiation in you, you can clear the mental and feeling world of others with whom you come in contact, and help them to hold to the constructive way of Life as well.

This is the reason We gave you the Use of Our Ascended Master Consciousness, because mankind's consciousness, left unillumined by the Ascended Masters' Consciousness, is nothing but the animal. You say, "Well, what about my Higher Mental Body?" You've had It all through the ages, and look at your depraved races in the World today. What do you think made them like that, if they had the full power necessary to keep from doing the destructive things that have made them what they are today?

Mankind needs to know of Our Existence and needs to call Our Life, Our Illumining Love into the emotional body, into the Heart Flame; and Our Illumining Wisdom, Our Illumining Power, Our Illumining Discrimination, and Our Illumining Intellect to keep mankind's consciousness from fooling itself.

Look at your so-called intelligentsia of the World today. What are they doing for mankind? They are using the good of the Universe to create more and more war, more and more confusion; and they are not setting the people free, and they are not telling them one word about the Ascension!

Now, where is the Illumining Consciousness that sets mankind free, if It doesn't come from the "Mighty I AM Presence" and the Ascended Host? *(applause)* Thank you so much, Precious Ones. Won't you be seated, please; and just remain so.

Before you start to do something, say to your "Beloved I AM Presence": "'*Mighty I AM Presence' and Beloved Seven Mighty Elohim, show me the Elohim Way to create this which I wish to do that is constructive! Fill me with*

*the Ascended Masters' Illumining Consciousness, and show me
the Ascended Masters' Way to do this, which fulfills the Divine Plan, to do whatever is constructive and hold it protected,
that it may bless others who pass this way!"*

Why, there is absolutely no limit to the Inspiration you can have, to the abilities that you can have
to do these things that are right, are constructive.
They should be done. They do fulfill the Divine
Plan. They are the sustaining of that which is right in
the Fulfillment of the Divine Plan in the physical
conditions of this physical world.

The Beloved Seven Mighty Elohim are the Givers of this Supreme Gift of Life. All I say to the mankind of this World is, "I challenge you to try it out
and see." *(applause)* Thank you so much.

Do you not think the mankind of this World
needs something to straighten out the chaos? Human
beings can't do it! Nations can't do it. Groups of
people can't do it. Education hasn't done it and can't
do it, and every other channel to which mankind
looks for assistance has not done it.

But anybody and any group of people, any individual or group of individuals that will call to the
"Beloved I AM Presence," the Ascended Host, and
especially to the Seven Mighty Elohim of Creation,
the Great Cosmic Beings, for the Illumining Intelligence that shows the outer intellectual consciousness

the right way to live Life, will receive the Direction and the Illumination, and will have the Victory over the hordes of evil that nothing else will bring! There isn't anything else to bring It!

Your Beloved Master Jesus is that Illumining Consciousness. Your Mighty Saint Germain is that Illumining Consciousness. Mighty Godfre is that Illumining Consciousness, and every Ascended Master and Cosmic Being!

When you call directly to the Seven Mighty Elohim of Creation, that is Our Hearts' Life inside of you that knows what you need, is given to you for the attainment of the Ascension, is the Protection of your own Life Stream of everything that is right, everything that is constructive, and is the ever-expanding Perfection and the way and means to create and produce and maintain and expand Perfection that is the Divine Plan's Fulfillment.

So, Blessed Ones, there is nothing you need to lack in this World when We are your Friends of the Light. We are your Friends of the Sacred Fire. We are your Friends of Eternity! *(applause)* Thank you so much.

Now, when you need to do something and you are not quite sure of yourself, or even sometimes when you go into a condition and you think you do know the right thing, don't be so sure of that! The human has been so trained and let to run wild and dash into everything, thinking it knows more than anybody else. Even when you think you know the right thing, stop a moment and *ask your "Beloved Mighty I AM Presence" and the Seven Mighty Elohim Heart Flame within you, to tell this outer self; blaze the Light and the Heart Flame of Indestructible Purifying Love through this outer self; possess it and control it, and prevent it from doing wrong!* You will avoid problems. You will avoid mistakes. You will avoid the things that have been your limitation and your distress down through the years.

Now when you do this, you will feel a Freedom you have never had before, because you will become aware that you can fill your world with Our Perfection, and you can control your world by Our Perfection; and then you will not need to depend on the conditions of the outer world that are here today and gone tomorrow, or that seem to be one thing, and when you have drawn them into your world, they have become the opposite of what they seemed.

This prevents mistakes, deception, and the trap of the sinister force to keep you from having the full Perfection of the Divine Plan fulfilled, and the full Mastery within yourselves to do that which is right, so long as you remain in this World.

If a thing seems to be right, still check it with your "Beloved I AM Presence" and with Us, and *ask*

Us to blaze Our Fiery Christ Truth, Our Fiery Christ Love, Wisdom, and Power, Our Fiery Christ Illumination, Our Fiery Christ Purity into this thing, to show you unmistakably what the Ascended Masters would do, what is the Ascended Masters' Way to do anything that seems constructive in the outer world, the Ascended Masters' Solution of a problem, your Ascended Masters' Correction of any mistake, the Ascended Masters' Removal of the opposition to the Fulfillment of the Divine Plan!

But you must *charge your own intellectual consciousness, and charge your feeling with Our Fiery Christ Alertness, Our Fiery Christ Love, Wisdom, and Power that holds absolute balance in the mind, in the feeling, in the substance of the things you handle, in the conditions in your world, so things do not get out of balance.* There isn't a human being in existence that can't have unlimited help, who will set this habit and hold to it, until it straightens everything out in the being and world of the outer self of the individuals who make the Call.

So, Blessed Ones, It is invaluable experience! How many people do you suppose in the World today, stop before they go into a thing and call to the "Beloved I AM Presence" and the Ascended Host to be filled with the Illumining Consciousness of Eternal Purity and Indestructible Perfection that shows the outer self the right thing to do?

Well, that is why We gave you the Use of Our Ascended Master Consciousness; and in that is all of everything that Life needs to know to create a World, or a System of Worlds, or Systems of Systems.

It's the same Consciousness that has been used throughout all time, past and present—and will through all time of the future—to produce any kind of manifestation that is constructive.

So when you want that which is constructive, when you want that which is right, *call to your "Beloved I AM Presence" and to the Seven Mighty Elohim Heart Flame within you, to come into you and fill this outer self with Our Sacred Fire Illumining Presence that won't let anything but what's right take place!* Then you will be free in no time! It won't let the outer self do things just to gratify the feeling of irritation against someone else. You will shut out the habits that have tortured you, and some of which you do not even know you have.

The anti-Christ is the deception of human feeling, and it is the accumulation of the mass discord of all mankind throughout the ages—the race consciousness of all human beings embodied in this World; and I assure you, you need protection against it.

So, even when you think you are right, still make your Call to your "Beloved I AM Presence" and set this habit to *call the Seven Mighty Elohim's Illumining Flame, Our Hearts' Flame, to fill you and make you the Victory of Ourselves in action, and blaze through you what prevents all wrong!*

Then, if you start to do something and it isn't right, your Higher Mental Body will check it, and Our Heart Flame will check it. If it is right, Our Heart Flame will protect it and help you to expand it. You cannot possibly make a mistake by using This; and if you don't do it, you will continue to make mistakes.

So, the Illumining Consciousness of the Seven Mighty Elohim of Creation is needed to do anything and everything that is the creation of Perfection, or of anything that is constructive in the physical world, as long as you remain here, unascended; and after you are Ascended, you will use It anyway; so you might as well get in the habit of doing it now—it is that much accomplished.

Blessed Ones, please believe Me tonight! Please use This to save yourselves problems and limitations from which you can just as well be free if you will do what I say tonight; but you've got to use the Heart Flame of the Seven Mighty Elohim inside of yourselves, and that is why We have been called the Seven Mighty Builders of Creation, the Seven Powers around the Throne. That is what is referred to in the Bible. It is the use, in everything you do, of Our Il-lumining Consciousness, of Our Fiery Christ Truth and Wisdom that We know you need, because We know a great deal more about you than you know about yourselves. And do you know something very encouraging? After you are Ascended, you won't want to know it. You won't want to remember it, because if you do, you'll make it Eternal, and I am quite sure you won't.

So don't be curious about what's in yourself. Just turn to your "Beloved I AM Presence" and the Ascended Host, and keep calling to Us to fill you with Our own Hearts' Flame of whatever We know prevents all wrong inside of you, and then blaze through you Our Hearts' Flame, all that We know prevents all wrong around you. And you are going to have to do this if you are going to keep disconnected from the discord of the outer world.

Then, if you will charge yourselves and your world with Our Seven Mighty Elohim Heart Flame Control of the condition around you, you will give your own "Beloved Mighty I AM Presence" and Higher Mental Body a chance to release Its own Life and Flame through you to produce the Perfection that holds the Divine Plan fulfilled, protects it, and frees you from human creation and human mistakes and human consciousness and human feeling. There is no other way, and that's why the Law of Life is such as It is.

This is the Divine Plan of Creation from the beginning of mankind's embodiment in this World; and that's why human beings have been reminded again and again and again in every age, "Call unto Me and I will answer thee!" Why do you suppose mankind was told to call unto Us, if We were not necessary?

Mankind is not nearly as self-sufficient as it thinks it is; and the day you get rid of the idea that the outer self is the doer and the knower and so on, you will find a peace you have never known before, because you are going to have to, someday, sometime, somewhere recognize, admit, and remember that the Heart Flame of Life is the Knower, the Giver, the Doer, the Manifester of every bit of Perfection in the Universe. And when you come to that point, then your intellect, the Flame in the Sevenfold Flame in the forehead, and the Heart Flame within the Heart become *one Flame*—and you become the Master of the Sacred Fire!

Beloved Ones, mankind has had so many suggestions poured to the intellect down through the ages, that the confusion is amazing—that's the only thing I have to say. And don't accept that old phrase, "No person is your friend, no one is your enemy, everybody is your teacher." Don't you believe it! The only teacher of Eternal Truth in the Universe there is, is your "Beloved I AM Presence" and the Ascended Host.

Anything in anybody that is constructive is the "Mighty I AM Presence" of that Life Stream. Every bit of anything constructive in anybody is the "Beloved I AM Presence," and that "Presence" must be given credit. Then, if you need the assistance of someone else that, perhaps, has poured more time and energy into learning something than you have, and that person knows the truth or is doing that which is constructive, well, then whatever is constructive there, is the Gift of the "Presence."

So don't give that human thing credit that belongs to the "Presence" or the Ascended Host. That's why the Mighty Saint Germain said to you in the beginning of this Instruction: "If in every thought, feeling, word, and act of the personal self, credit could be given to the 'Mighty I AM Presence' as the Doer, Miracles unbelievable would take place." I say the same thing to you tonight. If in everything you want to do, or that needs to be done or even that has been done, if it's a mistake, call Our Seven Mighty Elohim Sacred Fire's Indestructible Purifying Love, Wisdom, and Power into the condition, and the Violet Consuming Flame will consume the mistake.

When you ask for the Sacred Fire to go into a condition, It contains every Activity of the Sacred

Fire. It contains the Violet Consuming Flame, the Unfed Flame, the Sevenfold Flame of the Seven Mighty Elohim, and many other Activities of the Sacred Fire that, as yet, you do not use in the physical octave or do not understand.

No matter what has to be handled, the moment there is a problem to be handled, don't let the outer self dash into the problem. Turn it first to the "Mighty I AM Presence" and the Ascended Host, and call forth the Seven Mighty Elohim Control of the problem—but control yourself first. And when you have found the Master—when you feel Our Heart Flame's Mastery within you, you will find everything in the outer obedient to you, even to the Powers of Nature and Forces of the Elements.

So, Blessed Ones, I give you an Eternal Gift of Illumination tonight. I offer everything Our Hearts contain. I offer you not one thing that will ever produce discord in you or your world, and I offer you the Freedom of Eternity. And you cannot have the Mighty Saint Germain's Freedom in this World, Freedom from human creation, Freedom to take the Ascension until you recognize the Sevenfold Flame of the Seven Mighty Elohim in your forehead—and the Unfed Flame in your Heart and that Sevenfold Flame have been blended as One; and when you do, you will make no more mistakes.

You can just as well have that now as a year from now, or any other time. Please believe Me enough to try it out; and Our Hearts' Flame inside of you, will automatically prove Itself to you.

This is why each one of the Ascended Host, over months past, has turned the attention of the "I AM" Student Body again and again and again to the use of the Heart Flame, the Heart Authority, the Heart Command of Life, the Heart Control of Life, the Heart Victory over all in this World. We have given It to you again and again and again, in every way possible; and until individuals use It, they will be in limitation and distress and lack—until they do!

Now, I say one more thing. When you lack any good thing, please remember the Supply of every good thing is in the Heart Flame of your "Beloved I AM Presence" and the Heart Flames of the Seven Mighty Elohim of Creation, in the Heart Flames of the Ascended Masters and Cosmic Beings.

Everything that is given into this World is the Gift of the Heart Flames of those Great Cosmic Beings who have created this World, who sustain this World, who keep it in its orbit, who expand the Blessings and the Powers of Nature, that mankind may have the Blessings that Love has given.

Blessed Ones, if you care to clothe yourselves or ask Us to clothe you in Our Elohim Miracle Mantle of the Sevenfold Flame of Our Love's complete Control of manifestation—try it out! We are ready to prove the Reality of Our Existence! We are ready to prove the Power of Our Love in any condition in this World or any other; and Love will prove Itself the Master Presence of Creation.

The Gift We give is Eternal! It is the Mastery over all in this World. You have to have It before you can attain your Ascension; and It is the Blessing of the Power of Creation for Eternity, to create only that which is Perfection, forever expanding—and fulfills the Great Divine Plan. In Its use you can never make a mistake. I think it's time you came to that Freedom! *(applause)* Thank you. *There is no Freedom until you stop making mistakes.* So We are part of the Mighty Saint Germain's Freedom to this Nation and the World, Freedom to Life to attain the Ascension.

Blessed Ones, as I leave you enfolded in My own Heart's Flame of what We know will bring you the Fiery Christ Illumining Truth, Wisdom, Power, Memory, and every Faculty of Perfection within you, We enfold you and hold you in Our Miracle Mantle of Love's Mastery. And wherever you abide if you recognize this Miracle Mantle of Love's Mastery, you will know We are with you always. Accept It, use It, enter in, and have Its Victory over all in this World wherever you abide, until you come to Us for Eternity. Thank you with all My Heart.

(Record CD 1203)

CHAPTER V
Beloved Elohim Cyclopea

Shasta Springs, California
September 14, 1958

Beloved of My Heart, let us enter tonight into that deeper Understanding of Life that feels from the Heart of Creation, the Power of that Cosmic Christ Love within Life that is the Immortality of the Universe, that is the Strength and Power to do anything, and that is the Perfect Design of all Life's Perfection.

Tonight, if you will come with Me on a journey, I will give you a bird's eye view of what it means to watch the humanity of Earth over a long period of centuries, again and again and again choose suffering. Long have We waited for this Cycle to come in, wherein We could set aside the destructive use of the Free Will of mankind in this World enough to force the removal of the accumulated destruction and viciousness that has been imposed upon the Powers of Nature and imposed upon Life in this World.

This is truly a schoolroom of existence, and of course I need not tell you it's rather strenuous. But it's been strenuous for a long while, and now We see the dawn breaking in the east. We see the dawn of the New Day of the Violet Consuming Flame. May you dwell within Its Sunshine Presence and entering into the Great Powerhouse of the Universe, the Power of Transmutation, wherever you abide, call It into outer physical conditions and transmute everything you contact into something better, just for the sheer joy of doing it—because when you can learn to give the Perfection of Life everywhere just for the Joy of giving It, there will come into your outer use the Onrushing Perfection and Cosmic Flow of that which is to come into outer manifestation to fill the World, to fill you, and to be the raising Power that ever raises all manifestation to greater and greater Perfection.

I think sometimes you lose sight of the Action of Life. Because of your desire for something, you live in the future—or at least the contemplation of the future—in that intense feeling of desiring what you want. I would have you live in the *Eternal Now*, with the constant acknowledgment and demand and command and protection of Perfection made manifest now. This will give you some understanding of what it means to set aside the action of time and space.

As you recognize that there is no time so far as Cosmic Manifestations are concerned, and that time and space are but a mental concept, I would have you tonight, step through into Our Ascended Masters' Concept of Life's Instantaneous Action to Our Calls and Our Commands to Our Love, to Our Power to which there is no resistance.

Then, when you desire something that is the Fulfillment of the Great Divine Plan, you will find it coming instantly into being, into existence for your use. Then you will understand what it means to fill your beings and worlds with such Happiness, such Joyous Acknowledgment of the "Mighty I AM Presence" *present with you* in all of Its Release of Its Powers into your outer use, that you will understand that you may have anything and everything, so long as it be constructive and you have a right use for it, a constructive use for it. The "Mighty I AM Presence" and the Ascended Host not only are willing to release It, but It is ever flowing, seeking an opening through which It may be released into outer action.

So, your desire in your feeling world, when your desire is your love to your "Beloved I AM Presence," and your desire for Its Presence of Perfection in you and in the world around you is your constant feeling, it will not be long until your world takes on the Perfection of the "Presence" because Its Desire, if allowed to flow through you without obstruction, would bring you such happiness and would release such Power into your outer direction that you would simply fill your daily activities with those Manifestations of the Great Gifts of Cosmic Christ Love that you would flood into the outer world, for the sheer joy of manifesting it.

If people could only realize what Freedom, what Blessings can come by just always calling forth your own "Beloved I AM Presence'" eternally fulfilled Divine Desires for you, Divine Desires in you, Divine Desires around you! Then, My Dear Ones, you would give the "Mighty I AM Presence" and the Ascended Host a free rein in your outer affairs.

Now let Us come into a very practical use of This! Your very first Statement in *The "I AM" Discourses* says, "'I AM' is the Full Activity of God!" In other words, It is the Full Activity of Harmony, the Full Activity of Good. Then won't you take time enough in the morning as soon as you awaken, after pouring your love to your "Presence," you *ask your "Beloved I AM Presence" to fill*–now watch–*the world around you as well as yourselves with Its fulfilled Divine Desires manifest.* Now then, your world may contain may things that will pour Blessings to others, and sometimes you yourselves will hardly be aware of what your world can do for someone else. And in the Call for that to fill your world, *ask your "Beloved I AM Presence" to be Its fulfilled Management of all outer conditions by Its own Sacred Love of the Sacred Fire.*

Now, this has a double action; in asking your "Beloved I AM Presence" to pour This into the outer activities around you, you have kept yourself disconnected from the sense of strain and struggle. Your love to your "Beloved I AM Presence" keeps the Door open, keeps you harmonized so your "Beloved I AM Presence'" Divine Desires and Plans and Perfection and Management of you, in you, can get through. You see, your "Beloved I AM Presence" is all Powerful and so are We; but the Perfection which We are and which We offer must be drawn into you by your own Free Will and your love for that Perfection to come from the "Mighty I AM Presence" and Our Octave, instead of looking to the world without and trying to create your methods and ways and means of drawing from the outer world what it does not yet contain.

Now do you see where success lies? Do you see where Freedom is? So long as your attention is tied to physical channels, it is tied to limitation, for those channels are limited. But when you ask your "Beloved I AM Presence" to fulfill Its own Divine Desires in everything in your outer world experience, and hold Its Management of that creation around you, you have set up your world of Protection to start on. You have established, for that day, the Harmony and the Protection you will require, and then as you pour your love to your "I AM Presence" and ask It to come into you and hold Its Management in you, then you and your world will be harmonious, you and your world will cooperate, and you and your world will bless every particle of Life wherever you abide.

Sounds easy, doesn't it? It's much easier to live that way than your way. I know! I observe! I have beheld mankind's struggle a long, long time. I see the Perfection from within the Great Central Sun, and It is My Power of Sight that I have given to the Life Streams who have embodied in this World. If We did not see the Perfection of Life in the Manifestations of this World, what do you think would be the experience of the Life Streams who come into embodiment here to gain their Freedom?

If We did not hold the Picture of your Ascension for you, and if We did not plant within you the Action of Sight and the Desire, the Feeling within you to desire the Ascension, the Ascension as a Goal would not draw mankind into its Victory!

So, Blessed Ones, it is very imperative that you fill the world around you with the fulfilled Desires and Manifestations of your own "Beloved I AM Presence" for what It wants you to have! Then ask It to manage your outer world, *and* come in and manage you, inside of you—manage the inside of you.

You know what that is? That's the energy of your feeling world. And if you ask your "Mighty I AM Presence" to manage the feeling inside of you, I assure you, everything will be in Perfect Balance, everything will be under your control, because your "Beloved I AM Presence" in you, through Its Radiation, will *be* you in the outer. You didn't think you were going to lose your identity so soon, did you? *(applause)* Thank you so much.

The only identity you lose is that of struggle and limitation and problems. And I'm quite sure you might miss them for a while, but I'm sure you will not wish to call them back. Then as you move into outer physical conditions, you will find things moving into much more rapid Victory and Success; you come into the Instantaneous Release of these Powers, and you will have much greater capacity to help Life wherever you abide.

So, won't you let your "Beloved I AM Presence" and the Great Cosmic Beings who want to draw this Perfection into outer world conditions, have your cooperation and enable you to draw forth the Powers of more Instantaneous Fulfillment of everything that is a plan of construction, everything that is the Fulfillment of the Great Blessing to Life that must come into this World to redeem it?

Now if you will see within your minds tonight the World of Perfection as a Golden Sun, within which plays the Violet Consuming Flame; and as It comes into outer conditions to control them, hold the Picture in the intellect, in the outer self, of that which harmonizes conditions. Hold the Picture of that which blesses everyone. Hold the Picture of the Harmony you want. It is not difficult. My Dear Ones, I tell you truly, We live the easy way of Life and you live the difficult way. But if you will let Us manage your outer affairs, not only will Illumination come, not only will Happiness and Perfection come, but there will strengthen within you and within all Life that you contact—you will intensify the Strength of the Light in yourselves and in all, and that is the Raising Power of the Great Central Sun Magnet.

Now, We could intensify suddenly for the control of certain outer world conditions everything that is constructive in you, but We must have you protected against that which is discordant, for the increasing Power which We might need to use in a moment for the Blessing or Protection of others, would not be a strain upon you. For We do not do anything, even in an emergency, that would at any time be a strain upon anyone.

So, the Wisdom and the Management and the Directing Intelligence and Discrimination from within your Higher Mental Bodies and the Ascended Masters' Octave is what is needed in outer world conditions and outer world affairs to bring the God Solution into outer world conditions, instead of mankind changing one problem for simply a different kind of a problem, or maybe a dozen others.

Now, We must have you strengthened, My Dear Ones. We must have you protected. There is Work which We must do through you all; or rather, it is an Activity. And therefore in order to bring you to the use of this Power, We must have your worlds purified, harmonized, protected, and filled with as much of the Power and Perfection of your "Beloved I AM Presence" as you can draw forth in your Application in the very near future.

The outer world's continual turmoil in the feeling as well as in the mind, is a constant surge of energy just like the waves on the ocean. It is constantly swinging; and it swings one day one way, and it'll swing the opposite the next. There is no stabilization of it, except by the absolute Pressure of the Sacred Fire's Control of all energy. You have not quite understood that, as a matter of pressure to compel energy purified, harmonized, and balanced in outer world activities.

Now you many times call forth to ask the "Mighty I AM Presence" to show you the right thing to do. But I would explain the Law to you this way, and remind you to call forth from within your "Mighty I AM Presence" the Insight that you are going to require to know ahead what is the *right thing* to do, and then draw forth the Power and the Protection and the Strength to do it at the *right time* and in the *right way*. You need Insight, My Dear Ones. You need Discrimination; and you need to acknowledge often, *"'I AM' the Ascended Masters' Intelligence that makes me always know the right thing to do!"*

We offered you Our Ascended Master Consciousness. We offered you the Sacred Fire of Our Love. We've offered you the Assistance of the Great Angelic Host. Now We offer you Our Directing Intelligence and Insight, because if you are going to allow your "Beloved I AM Presence'" Divine Desires, fulfilled and manifested, come into your outer world activities, then you need Its Directing Intelligence and Insight. You need to know ahead how to anticipate that which you will next need to do, and draw the Power with which to do it.

So, Beloved Ones, Ascended Master Management—which contains all of This—is a very, very practical Action of Life. So, if before you have to manage anything, even including yourselves, you simply send that Flame of Love to your "Presence" and ask It to blaze Its Management in you, Its Control in you, Its

Almighty Protection into you and your world, and at all times, through you, do that which you need to have done—the next thing you need to know. Call for Illumination. Call for Directing Intelligence. Call for Discrimination, because if most people had more discrimination they would not make the mistakes they do. And for your Blessing and the Blessing of all Life everywhere, call forth—for I offer This to you with all the Love of My Heart—*call forth My Cosmic Power of Silence*.

My Cosmic Power of Silence is an Action within the mind as well as through the eyes. It's an Action of knowing and comprehending and seeing what is the next thing to do to produce Perfection. But in the assistance which needs to come now to the people of the outer world in the actual, physical use of physical sight, this Power which it is My Privilege to bestow upon the Life Streams who come into this World, needs to be drawn into outer world conditions to perfect the physical sight, to perfect the Comprehending Consciousness within the mind. And three quarters of that Comprehending Consciousness is within your feeling. That acts through the Heart, and through the intellect, and through the Power of Sight.

Because of the interference with the physical sight of so many of the people of the World, as you *call My Cosmic Power of Sight, Inner and outer, to purify and perfect the Sight and the Power of Seeing in all Life,* it will enable Me to at all times send to you or through you, the Pictures from the Inner Level of the Perfection that is to come into the Incoming Civilization. Now don't go off on a wild tangent and, every time you see something from the Inner, imagine that that's the Perfection from the Ascended Masters' Octave. Unless it is Perfection, do not accept it! If you call for My Power of Perfect Sight, Inner and outer, to clear the comprehension of mankind, to perfect their sight that all may see the Perfection that is to come, then you will in your Call as a Blessing to the rest of Life— you will have that Perfection within yourselves.

So, Blessed Ones, the Power of the All-Seeing Eye of God is of tremendous import to Life everywhere, because It begins with the Comprehending Consciousness within the individual to understand. And then, as the Pictures are held within the mind, and the feelings love those Pictures of Perfection, that Feeling is the Drawing Power that lowers That into your outer use.

Blessed Ones, heretofore you have built things in your world by gathering outer world conditions and things together, and you placed them together and built what you call your modern civilization. I am offering you the Ascended Masters' Way of producing Manifestation! This time, if you will reach into the Sun Presence of your "Beloved I AM" and reach into Our Octave to draw forth these Qualities and Powers and Manifestations of Life, you will draw Our Perfection, and create in this World and lower into outer world conditions the Perfection We have already waiting for you!

Beloved Ones, It will bring you Blessings without limit, and It will be the reversal of the old habits of looking to the outer and feeling that only the things that you see and can feel are real. We might seem to be Invisible, but not nearly so much so as mankind believes, and We are far more tangible than anyone understands.

As your Beloved Saint Germain has told you again and again, *do not look to outer conditions for what you require, but turn constantly to your "I AM Presence" and expect everything from there, and expect It to give you what It knows you are going to require;* and when that is the first thing you do, then whatever you do in the physical world will automatically be the right thing to cooperate with what is coming from within. Then you bring into outer world conditions, perhaps things that have never been here before, but things far in advance of what mankind has today.

If you *call for That to be always Invincibly Protected against all that is of the sinister force,* whatever you draw into outer use no destructive force can touch, no one can take it from you, and it will never give you one instant of unhappiness. That is why I plead for all of you to make your Calls constantly to your "Presence," send your love there, ask the "Presence" to come into you, ask the "Presence" to manage your world. Ask the "Presence" to give you what It knows you are going to require. Then, you not only will have your struggle cease, but you won't have problems, because what comes from your "Presence" into your outer use will only produce Harmony and Perfection that blesses all and brings Freedom to all you contact.

So, to live in the habit of drawing from Our Octave of Life the Perfection that is the next thing to be drawn into outer world conditions, will enable you to disconnect your attention from the old methods of gaining things from the outer world. And since the outer world is in such chaos and it is so uncertain, I offer you the absolute Security that you hear so much about, and of which you have so little. All this security talk in the outer world–there is nothing secure in the outer world, except constant change.

Beloved Ones, We are offering you the Supreme Cosmic Insurance of Life. I sound commercial tonight, do I not? *(applause)* Thank you so much.

I assure you, you'll never have a loss in the kind of Security that We offer. Your only loss will be that of your human creations, and I'm sure you'll want to part with them. If you ever had a glimpse for just a few seconds, or one minute, into the Realm of your own "Beloved I AM Presence'" Cosmic Activities, into the Realm of the Ascended Masters' Octave, into Our Temples of the Sacred Fire, and could see the Powers that are used to produce Perfection—just three or four seconds or a half a minute observing That, would be an experience within you, you could never forget. And more than that, it would be a Magnet within you to draw That into outer world activities that you might give It for the Freedom of Life.

So, Blessed Ones, We are reversing the trial and error method, and I think you have had more error than you have had trial almost. *(laughter)* So, let Us close the door, and let's just try for a while—just experiment for a few days with this, of calling Ascended Master Management into your outer world conditions. But manage yourselves first. *Call Ascended Master Management into yourselves to manage everything within you,* because the Ascended Masters' Management will not allow anything to be out of Balance.

Now, this will be of a most Illumining Activity within you. You ask Us to manage you, but you must cooperate with Us by placing your "Beloved I AM

Presence" first and then holding the feeling quiet; and as soon as that Stillness comes within you, the Door is open. Your Higher Mental Body's Faculties, just as clear as crystal, will fill the outer intellect with that which you next require and will give you the reasonable explanation of everything. Your mental confusion will be gone. Your comprehension will be infinitely more rapid and complete. You will see the Pictures that will bring you great Joy, and you will lower those Activities into outer use to bless your fellowman.

Oh, Beloved Ones, We want you free, so much. We want you free more than you want that Freedom! You don't quite believe that, but that's true; for We know the Happiness and Freedom and Power in Our World of Activity. In Our Great Octave of Existence, We know the Perfection that is there! We behold the imperfection that is here. And only when you enter into the Realm of Light will you understand what the Treasure-house of the "Mighty I AM Presence" contains, and then will you know what All-Power means. Just as certainly as you draw This within yourselves and draw It into your outer world affairs, will you find Us very much closer with you; and you will find many, many Powers coming into your outer use that will bless you without limit, and through which you may bless others.

If you will experiment with calling forth Our Powers of Inner Sight and Inner Hearing and the Inner Music, you cannot help but be harmonized. When this clear Inner Sight comes into you, you *comprehend* quickly and completely that which you wish to know, and then you *see* that Perfection out here. Then you *hear* the Music at the Inner Realms of Activity. *You have the Comprehension, the Picture, and the Sound,* which is the Feeling. If you will combine these three, you will have Joy unspeakable, and Freedom will really begin to fill you and your world; and you will know what it means to enter into the Use of the Powers that have long been yours, have awaited your use, and can but bless you and all the rest of Life.

Now, for the Blessing of your fellowman, if you will *call forth whatever Sacred Fire brings Illumination and Purity into the outer faculties of mankind, and demand the Perfection of the sight and the hearing and the comprehension of the mental and feeling world of mankind,* if you'll give that Blessing to the rest of Life, automatically within your world—within you—will come the greater Perfection also. So, in order to safeguard your own Powers of Sight and Comprehension, your Powers of Hearing, your Powers of Feeling, the Power of your Attention, as you hold This within yourselves, and you ask for This to come forth through all Life and clear the consciousness of mankind so all individuals may behold Our Visible, Tangible Presence—just as certainly as you make that Call to give that Help to the rest of Life, will you automatically have It within yourselves.

So, Blessed Ones, wherever you go, you may lift mankind's distress, you may see the shadows disappear, and you may dwell in the Sunshine of Our Happiness; for just as certainly as you help Us to help mankind be free, will the Cosmic Law permit Us to give Our greater Blessings to help you, and you cannot give without receiving. We want you to receive the Perfection from Our World that It may begin to grow in this World, and not only bless you, but It becomes a Release of the Powers of Nature and Forces of the Elements quite as well as the Release of mankind from the struggle and strain and uncertainty of the past.

Now, one more thing. If I were you I would definitely demand my release from all doubt and all fear. These are the two feelings within individuals— they are both feelings—and you have no idea how many, many, many forms they take to keep mankind enslaved to the destructive forces of the sinister force.

So, Beloved Ones, if you absolutely *demand your Complete and Eternal Release from all doubt and all fear, and you demand mankind's release from all doubt and all fear,* it will give Us an opportunity to use certain Cosmic Powers of the Sacred Fire and Illumination that, I assure you, will release a Light through the feeling world of mankind, and you will see the shadows roll back like sooty smoke in the atmosphere. And as the Light comes in, that substance that has been in the mental and feeling world of mankind for so long will leave the individual, and will be consumed as it leaves the atmosphere of Earth. And it is—the doubt and the fear are feelings that have enslaved millions of Life Streams through the centuries, and We would like to see them set free.

If I were you, I would certainly *demand whatever Cosmic Christ Power annihilates all doubt and fear in your own world and then from mankind, and take it away from all Life*. Take it away even from the animal creation, for if you were to remove the fear in animals, you would remove their destructive, vicious qualities. You have no idea what feelings have done to Life.

One more thing I would offer to help you, and that is, if you *call forth the Ascended Masters' All-Powerful Master Control of your attention,* it would—just automatically like a needle jumping to the magnet would— automatically turn to your "Presence" and to Us, and you would draw from Our World everything you could use long before the outer world will receive it.

Then you must be very careful not to brag about it, not to exploit it, and in many cases not to even tell anyone about it. But go on, dwell within It, use Its Powers, give Its Blessings and let your deeds speak for themselves. And My Dear Ones, you have no idea what Mastery comes from the complete control of your attention, your feeling, and your power of sight; and when you are released from the vibratory action of doubt and fear, you will know what it means to be in the world but not of it, and you will feel a Mastery that will never come in any other way. Mastery is the Balanced Control of Energy, and it's the Purification that keeps everything harmonized.

So, when you have asked for your release from all doubt and all fear, hold the attention upon your "Beloved I AM Presence" and Our Great Octave of Life, and ask for Our Perfection, Our World to come into your world; and do you know what will happen? We pour down the Sacred Fire and Cosmic Light Rays that raise the vibratory action of your world. And when your world is increased to the Vibratory Action of Ours, no evil thing can exist or remain. It is the Harmonious, Eternal, All-Masterful Way of controlling everything in manifestation and redeeming the World from that which has been imposed upon it.

So come with Me, if you will, and you will find the Seven Mighty Elohim your elder Brothers in the Great Creative Activities of the Universe; and as the builders of the Incoming Perfection, you will know a Joy that knows no bounds, you will feel you have come home, and then Love will claim its own. You won't want to send out anything except that which produces greater Perfection. And when you dwell with Us in This, you will have forgotten how to be discordant. Do you not think it's worth every effort you could make to reach into this Powerhouse for which We are calling, that you may have It for use in your outer world affairs, and you can dwell in the Security and Love and Power of the House of the Almighty. *(applause)* Thank you so much, Precious Ones. And may My Heart's Love ever pour to you the Desire and Strength in that Desire, and give you the Power to attain this as quickly as possible. Thank you; and won't you be seated, please.

Now in that Service which the Seven Mighty Elohim are constantly rendering to Life, you do not quite realize just how closely you are connected with Our Life Streams; and yet, the Unfed Flame in your Heart and the Sevenfold Flame in your forehead are the Sacred Fire Presence of Our Life in you. May you feel It and know It, and let It expand until It has consumed everything that is not Our World of Perfection forever. Therefore, Our Love abides with you, and gives you the Strength and the Power and the Protection that does fulfill your Calls.

May you have Victory without limit, and Freedom will be yours for Eternity. Just give Our Perfection to Life everywhere, and you and We will be *One* in the Perfection and Manifestations that must come to fill this World; and everything you do will glorify your "Mighty I AM Presence," will glorify your Nation, will glorify your fellowman, will glorify the Universe because you have passed this way. There is nothing superior to That, and it is worth every effort you will ever make!

Tonight, I want to leave with you the Desire, the Strength, the Power, and the Protection for you to accomplish this, that you may know the greatest Joy you have yet experienced; and wherever you abide It forever expands to the rest of the universe around you.

Thank you with all My Heart for Eternity.

(Record CD 556AB)

Excerpts on the All-Seeing Eye

Beloved Cyclopea

Tonight, I hope you will call forth all the Power of the All-Seeing Eye in the North Wall of the Royal Teton. That was placed in this Nation in the beginning as a Focus of the Eternal Sacred Fire Sustaining Perfection for this portion of the World.

(Cassette SGC 285, side 2)

Beloved Lanto

Since the All-Seeing Eye of God's Activities is permanently established in the Retreat of the Royal Teton to pour forth Its Cosmic Rays and Action of the Flame throughout the centuries, then from the Inner Standpoint, I would like to have you see that the All-Seeing Eye of God is the Consciousness of Light that has watched over America, and which still watches.

The Power of that Eye, heretofore, was only released once in a hundred years. Under the Action of the Cosmic Law, It has been pouring forth Its Purifying Activities once in six months. Now you can see the proportion, or increase, with which the Cosmic Law acts, in comparison to that Cycle wherein the Law of the individual's Free Will was paramount.

("Voice of the I AM," January 1990)

Beloved Lanto

When you understand that every Activity of the Sacred Fire or the Cosmic Light is some Life Stream's Love to the rest of Life, you will know what it means to draw forth into the physical conditions of this World the Purifying Love of the Sacred Fire, the Purifying Love of the Great Great Silence, and the Purifying Love of every Retreat of the Ascended Masters throughout the World! . . .

. . . So it is tonight, when the Mighty Cosmic Presence of Beloved Cyclopea draws forth from the Physical Sun and the Great Central Sun, the Mighty Light Rays that are to go forth through the Great Eye in the North Wall of the Royal Teton. When that Mighty Stream of Electronic Force is poured forth to various places in the Nation and the World, try to realize that It is Love illumining the atmosphere of the Nation and the World. It is the Love of His Mighty Life Stream pouring forth That which is constructive throughout the World, and It is the Illumining Presence of everything that is constructive, which He draws forth from the Great Central Sun; and so can it be with you.

("Voice of the I AM," December 1983)

CHAPTER VI
Beloved Elohim Cyclopea

Los Angeles, California
November 2, 1958

Beloved of the Light, as We give an explanation this hour of what your activities are producing from the Inner Level, I hope you will understand the privilege that is yours, and the Power you have to set into action the many Powers of the Cosmic Law's Blessing to the Earth, through the Activities of the Sacred Fire and Cosmic Light-Substance.

I want to explain something so that each of you knows what is being done when you hold a Picture of one or more of the Ascended Host, or the Cosmic Beings, or you hold the Picture of a Sun Presence, the Heart Presence, or a Star Presence of these Activities from the Heights of Eternal Perfection.

Do not ever allow your intellect to say, "Well, I can't visualize." You are using pictures every waking moment, with your eyes open or shut; and you are using pictures every moment the physical body is asleep. There is no time that the All-Seeing Eye of God is not acting through Life everywhere. Therefore, when you are in physical embodiment, the control of the power of vision within the mind, or through the, what you call the physical sight—through the eyes—your power of vision is acting through you to contact that which is in the world of manifestation around you.

Therefore, you are creating and building and photographing upon yourselves some form of life all the time. You have a discriminating faculty; and if you do not refuse to see that which is destructive, then it's going to come into you. And if it be destructive and you take it into yourselves, it's going to destroy you. You can't fool with the Law of Energy and Vibration.

Everything in manifestation is producing an effect upon Life, upon substance, upon energy everywhere. Therefore, it is your responsibility to take control of your mind, take control of your attention, hold control of your feeling—which means the energy of your emotional body—and definitely direct, create, and hold the Picture of the Perfection you want, and absolutely forbid a picture of something you do not want to come to your attention.

Now, you are the *deciding intelligence* as to what you want to contemplate within your being and world, what you want to manifest in the world around you. Now, the mass habit in the race consciousness of mankind, through doubt and fear, is to consciously and constantly outpicture evil—something that is destructive or distorted or not perfect.

Therefore, if you want Perfection, you must hold the Picture of Perfection. Now, this faculty acts, the power of sight acts through the physical eyes; but it also acts within the mind, because the consciousness of you—your consciousness of Life—is the intelligence within you to see that which you want to create or produce in outer manifestation. And you even have the expression, when someone explains something to you, your expression is, "Oh, I see what you mean." In other words you comprehend, the mind within comprehends what some other intelligence of Life is giving you to use within yourselves.

Now, the outer world and the Infinite Universe around you is filled with Miracles of Perfection, is filled with Magnificent Manifestations of Beauty and the Creation of the Great Cosmic Beings who have given Their boundless Blessings to the mankind of this World, to experience in the use of the Power of Life, to use all things constructively, and go forward to the attainment of the Ascension.

Now, when your "Mighty I AM Presence" sees you are determined to hold a Picture of Perfection, whether it be for yourselves or the Nation or the World, or just to bless Life everywhere, matters not;

the moment you have decided to hold a Picture of
Perfection and you make that a habit in the intellect
of seeing that Picture again and again and again;
when you have given a certain amount of the energy
of your Life into that Picture, which is your mental
thought-form—if it be constructive then your Higher
Mental Body and one or more of the Ascended Host,
the Angelic Host, will take up that constructive Picture and, pouring into it the Substance from the Ascended Masters' Octave and the Sacred Fire of the
Life of those Beings who are assisting you, They will
make that thought-form or the Picture you are holding a living, pulsating creation, a living, pulsating
thing in your own atmosphere, like a mighty genera-
tor or storage battery, to hold in your atmosphere the
Ascended Masters' Power of the Sacred Fire and Substance of Light, and Their Directing Intelligence,
Love, and Perfection to constantly produce for you
that which will assist you to create and produce Perfection to bless Life.

     If this be charged with protection, that stands as
a living thing in your atmosphere; and you may
make that as Invincibly All-Powerful as you desire.
I am speaking of this all on the constructive side, because when you create something constructive, and
by conscious pre-determination and habit, give that
your Life again and again and again by holding the

Picture within your world, then you can create a Sun Presence of that Power in and around the physical body. Then the Ascended Masters or Cosmic Beings to whom you call will ever add Their Sacred Fire and Love and Substance, Their Intelligence from Their Octave into yours. And that becomes an eternal part of your Life Stream. That becomes the Ascended Masters' Power in you and your world, to create and produce greater good. And that is why in the beginning of this "I AM" Activity, the Blessed Saint Germain said to you, "We offer you the use of Our Ascended Master Consciousness."

So, when you want Ascended Master Power or Powers to use in the physical octave to produce Perfection in this World, then you must hold the Picture. And then your Higher Mental Body and We can co-operate, create the Sun Presence of what you desire, anchor It in and around you; and It becomes the Protection around you that will hold Protection for all that is constructive.

I am keeping this entirely on the constructive side of Life, because through habit you may increase the release of the energy in any particular activity to any degree whatsoever. There's no limit to the amount of energy that you can have to create anything constructive; and if you will demand it be Invincible against everything else forever, you will find the Manifestations for which you call not only coming into outer physical conditions, but you will find them made Invincible against destruction. Then if you stood among the wreck of a world, that which you have created that is of God would be Invincible and untouched by the destructive activities of mankind's discord.

Now, you can absolutely hold this Invincible Sun Presence of the Purifying Freedom of God to this Nation, enfolding the Nation in a Violet Flaming Sun Presence, demanding Its Invincible Protection to all that is of God within your borders. If you will hold this Picture and charge it day after day with your Life, We too will charge it day after day with Our Life, Our Sacred Fire Invincible Freedom, Our Sacred Fire's Love for Freedom, Our Sacred Fire's Protection of Freedom, that Life may no longer be bound by the discord of human generation.

Habit, My Dear Ones, is but an accumulation of energy—be it good or otherwise. And therefore, these creative faculties which you have of the mind and the feeling—in which I am extremely interested, and am the Authority in the mankind of this World—you may use at this hour to bring Protection to all that is of God, all that is constructive everywhere.

So, Blessed Ones, there's no such thing as a person being without help in this Universe; and I want

you to feel that tonight with everything you are and
have. Don't ever allow a feeling to come into you
that you're helpless before destructive forces. Once
you know of your "Beloved I AM Presence," once
you know you can command with your Life and use
the Great Creative Word, "I AM", give the Great
Command of Life for God's Manifestation, for God's
Power, for God's Perfection, for God's Control to
come into all physical conditions—oh, if you only
know what Power you have to command as We
command, you would manifest as We manifest; and I
must be that Courage for you tonight. It must come!
(applause) Thank you so much, Precious Ones. And
so long as you command *God made manifest,* God will
manifest to you.

Now, you've done plenty of commanding on
the negative side of Life; you've acknowledged conditions of limitation down through the centuries. From
now on I ask you, regardless of all appearances, to
command and command and command, and continue to command in yourselves and around you the
God-Manifestations of Ascended Master Protection
and Victory over all evil.

Now, in doing this you build a Powerhouse in
and around yourselves of your own Life, your own
energy, which We will amplify without limit until
you can be absolutely Invincible against everything

that is a destructive force. Then you move in the world, but not of it; and yet you have power unlimited to give protection to all that is constructive everywhere. And if you keep the habit established of picturizing only that which is God made manifest, good made manifest, constructive activity made manifest—then We automatically have a free hand to amplify that without limit, and give you anything and everything from Our Octave that enables the Power of Protection and Perfection to hold command and control of all within your Nation and all throughout the World.

I am stressing this with all the Power you can stand tonight, because the hordes of evil have, through continued misuse of the energy, accumulated more and more power, qualified with destructive qualities and with destructive intent, to try to prevent mankind creating the Protection and Perfection of God that does fulfill the Divine Plan of Life.

Now We, in Our Ascended Masters' Octave of Life, cannot and will not and do not protect evil. It cannot be. So, unless a thing be constructive, We cannot allow mankind to have Our Energy and Our Life to produce manifestation down here; but with all the Blessings and with all the Good that has been given to the people of this World down through age after age after age, that good has not been made

Invincible against evil. Therefore, it has dissolved and disappeared.

You are in the Cycle now when everything that comes onto this Earth in the future—and not too far distant future—must be made Invincible against evil, or We cannot give It. So, regardless of what conditions you want to see changed in the outer world, *when you call forth anything that is good, don't fail to demand that it be made Cosmically Invincible against all evil forever.* Then, My Dear Ones, you will never be caught in the trap of the sinister force to enslave you or deprave you or get you connected with something that is destructive.

This of which I speak is Invincible Protection to you forever, by the Power of God from Our Octave of great Mastery. Now, this is what it means to bear witness to the Truth, and to live to glorify the "Mighty I AM Presence" by using It—all that is in the Universe—to produce constructive manifestations that first of all flood you and your world, because it's your Life. And then, as We sustain it and protect it and expand that, it gives Its Blessings to all Life around you. And you become a Powerhouse. You become a Sun Presence. You'll become the Master Authority and Power of the Sacred Fire of Life to create and produce Perfection, Invincible for Eternity; and then in your world of change, the quality is ever

Perfection and the quantity forever expands. And thus are Systems of Worlds created.

You are a co-creator with the Beings in the Great Central Sun. Therefore, you are held responsible for all creative activities of Life that touch your Life. Do you not see how—because you have Free Will—you are able to be the Master Presence that does control conditions in the world around you. Then you can be of infinite help to your Nation and infinite help to Life; and then as you serve Life for your Freedom, you know no longer the problems of distress and limitation. You no longer struggle in the discord of mankind's creation; but you stand the Powerhouse, a Sun Presence of the Love from the Heart of Creation, endowed with every constructive activity you could ever desire; and using everything in infinite space at your Call, you may create here the Perfection that is There. And you go on and on and on with the Magnificent Power of Mastery, and interference you know not longer.

This is the Divine Way to live Life. It begins by your correction within yourselves of your own use of your faculties of creation; and therefore, your first Discipline within is the control of your attention, because without placing your attention upon the Source of Perfection, the Power of Perfection, the Sacred Fire of Perfection, the Substance of Perfection which the

Light is and the Sacred Fire is—unless your attention goes There, holds the picture There, pours the love There and draws that back into yourself or into your world, unless you control your creative powers, how can you manifest the Perfection for which you call?

Now, mankind has held the attention upon the miscreations and distress of the outer world; and therefore, the outer self is tied to that distress. If you want your Freedom, if you want the Purifying Freedom of Life, your attention must go to your "Mighty I AM Presence" and the Ascended Host and the Angelic Host; your love, your feeling, your energy must go to your "Beloved I AM Presence" and the Ascended Host.

Your Call must go to the Source of Perfection of your "Mighty I AM Presence" and the Ascended Host. You must go back to the Source from whence you came—the Great Central Sun—and there the Pattern of Perfection, there the Power of Love Supreme, there the Infinite Purity of Creation, there the Boundless Energy of the Universe, there the Boundless Supply of all substance, can you draw back into yourselves; and then you give your Life to the world around you, and It produces only Perfection that blesses Life. You dwell only within Its Perfection. You command Its Expansion. You demand Its Invincible Power against all evil; and you become the

Great Central Sun's Magnetic Raising Force, the
Great Central Sun Magnet's Power, to raise and raise
and raise all you contact into that same great Perfection to which you have called, to which you belong,
from whence you came, and to which you must return.

Oh, the Seven Mighty Elohim are so ready to
give you everything! We are the Builders of the System. Think you not We can build Perfection for
you? But you must become *One* with Us. Since We
build Perfection, and you want to build Perfection,
you must become *One* with Us; and you must build as
We build. Perfection does not come from the outer
world. It comes from what the world calls the
"invisible"; and yet, it is not invisible. It's far more
visible than many of your manifestations in the
physical octave that are here one minute and gone the
next. This is the world of eternal change; therefore,
let Us change it from its present distress, so far as
you're concerned, into the Sun Presence of the Perfection of your "Mighty I AM Presence," the Perfection of the Ascended Masters' Octave, the Perfection
of the Seven Mighty Elohim of Creation.

These Powers are ever within Life. We are
ever offering Them to you. They are seeking an
opening. They ever bless and fill all with the Happiness of Eternity, the Mastery of Manifestation, and

They glorify everything you contact. Can I offer you
more? And can the world offer you as much?

The World needs this of which I speak, and
you are able to give it. You have given much; you
can give more. And may I say tonight, you *will* give
more! *(applause)* Thank you so much, Precious Ones.
Won't you be seated, please; and just remain so.

Now Blessed Ones, as you school yourselves
and set this habit, and you begin to create this Sun
Presence of greater Perfection and Purifying Freedom
to Life, as you draw more Power into yourselves, as
you demand more Power to purify and free the Life
around you, We will add to That. So your Power
increases more and more rapidly. But only as you
increase It to give It out here, can We pour the
greater Power into you and make you more powerful, make you a more intense Sun Presence of the
greater Power from Our Octave.

So, the greater Power in you of Mastery depends on the greater Power of Blessing that you give
to Life around you. And there's no substitute for
blessing Life. This Messenger has three times today
had a quite amazing experience, and she tries it many
times just to see the reaction: People of the outer
world, just the general run of people, when she has
said, "God bless you for a miracle day," there's instantly an awakening, instantly a smile, instantly a

response; and she receives, "Oh, thank you!" Now what do you think is that action to Life? Beloved Saint Germain told you in the early days, that something very wonderful was established in and around you when you form the habit of just saying, "God bless you!" and meaning it.

As That goes out to touch Life, you have no idea the burdens you lift; and it is so easy to do. There's nothing difficult. It's not complicated, but you must desire to give It. And when that is your desire, Our Desire can be fulfilled in you and through you, and Our Desire for the World to be free comes more quickly into outer fulfillment.

So, Blessed Ones, there's no substitute for the Blessing to Life. Just enjoy it; and if you will give It, We can give to you the Boundless Blessings of Our Octave. Then your world becomes the Ascended Master World of Perfection; and wherever you abide, you are the Magnetic Raising Power of the Great Central Sun Magnet's Blessing to Life. When the greater Life of the Universe is so ready to raise the lesser Life into the greater Freedom and Perfection of the greater Realms of Activity, there's no excuse for staying in the disturbed, tormenting, traitorous, treacherous, limiting conditions of human discord.

So, Blessed Ones, you are the Purifying Freedom of the Sacred Fire's Love to Life when you use

that Violet Consuming Flame, when you call forth
the Inner Essence of any special activity, when you
hold your attention through love to your "Mighty
I AM Presence," and you call and call and call to the
greater Realms of Life, the greater Perfection and
greater Power of the Universe, you yourself through
the Call, become the Open Door through which We
can pour into you and into this World that which
needs to come here to raise it out of the clutches of
the destructive forces of mankind's own human creation.

　　We create only Perfection.   We protect only
that which is constructive. We give only the Good of
Life; and it is all as free as the air you breathe. Can
the world do as much for you? Has the world done
as much for you? Then let Us do for the world what
is necessary now to enable the world to do for
the Universe around it that which We do and offer,
and which the Cosmic Law demands until that
hour when all purified, manifests the Perfection of the
Ascended Masters' Great Freedom of Life, and the
Great Creative Activities of the Universe go on and
on and on in greater Magnificence and Beauty,
greater Power without limit, and are made invincibly Eternal in the ever-expanding Perfection of
manifestation.

So, Blessed Ones, I hope I have brought you Courage this afternoon. I trust I have encouraged you; and if you will let Me have your problems and your struggle, you will find My World a lovely place to live. You will find the Great Creative Activities of the Seven Mighty Elohim of Creation bringing Their Blessings into you and the world around you; and as builders of the Incoming Civilization, you will glorify your "Beloved I AM Presence" and the Mighty Saint Germain who has opened the Door to help you through to Freedom. This is what the Master Jesus meant when He said, "'I AM' the Open Door that no man can shut," because not all mankind put together can prevent you loving your "I AM Presence" in the Silence, in your feelings, and using the Conscious Command of Life to produce the Perfection that is Freedom for all.

None can interfere with your Free Will to do that; and you have been endowed by the Great Law of Embodiment from the Great Central Sun, you have been endowed with the Great Creative Powers of Life, and They are yours to use as free as the air you breathe; but you must use Them. You must become the Sun Presence of that Eternal Perfection that is Master everywhere. Then, when manifestation of discord appears, if you have gained the momentum of this Power in and around you, you can but speak the

Word, and no weapon prospers against you—be it in mankind, the Powers of Nature, or Forces of the Elements.

Fail not to use that Statement, "No weapon prospers against the Christ." The Christ is all that is constructive. And if you stand within that, you face and conquer everything unlike It, because It is the Master Presence, the Master Authority, the Master Intelligence, the Master Command of all the infinite created Universe. You surely are not without friends. You certainly are not without hope; and there's no such thing as failure for you if you choose to dwell in My World with Me by this Conscious Command— and I trust you will. *(applause)* Thank you so much. In these few minutes I've been with you, I've given you many Secrets of Life; and if you will use them, they will teach you of themselves. And as they teach you, you will become that which is Master of all.

So go forward. Use them! Enjoy them! And why not take your Stand from this hour, that from this hour by Our Sacred Fire Command to Life, you are free from all problems, all struggle, all mistakes, all limitations. Why not leave them behind and come with Me? *(applause)* Thank you so much. I have watched you a long time. *"I AM" the All-Seeing Eye of God!* You ever live under the Watchful Eye of that Mighty Intelligence of the "I AM Presence" and the

Great Beings from the Central Sun, from whom nothing is hidden, who are the Masters of all, the Givers of all, and the Saving of all.

If you care to acknowledge and see and feel the Sun Presence of Our Great Sacred Fire Power of Light in and around yourselves, We will dwell with you and within you; and wherever you abide We will abide also. And where We are, no evil can ever come near you. That is the World I offer you in the midst of the chaos of outer shadows. And in this you will become the Sun Presence in which no shadows can ever exist, which no shadows can ever touch; and you will no longer feel anything but the Purifying Freedom of the Eternal Light.

May My Love enfold you and be a Garment about you. May the Sacred Fire Presence of the Seven Mighty Elohim produce for you the Manifestations of Perfection Indescribable, Invincible, Almighty for Eternity; and let you go forward and hold the balance wherever you abide. And you, facing the Light, become the Light of the World; and that which you once feared will flee at your approach, and you will no longer doubt the Instantaneous Answers to your Calls.

So Blessed Ones, with all the Love, all the Good, all the Power that is of Perfection without limit, We flood to you this hour; and may each of you be a Sun Presence of Its complete Mastery over this World, and your Purifying Freedom lift your fellowman onto the Pathway of Light where each one sees the Goal unto the Ascension, and no longer can shadows cross your pathway.

"I AM" the *All-Seeing Eye of God to the Earth,* from whom nothing is hidden, and whom you must one day face; and when you come face to face with that which I am, you will find we are *One!*

In the Fullness of that Enfolding Sacred Fire Presence and Consciousness and Intelligence of Life, I enfold you unto the Fullness of your Eternal Victory in the Ascension. And may the Peace of that Love that passeth understanding go forth from you this hour, and still the turmoil of the World wherever you abide, heal all, give all, and protect all unto the Fullness of the Attainment of the Final Victory into the Ascended Masters' Octave. Thank you with all My Heart.

(Record CD 1661)

CHAPTER VII
Beloved Elohim of Peace

Santa Fe, New Mexico
April 20, 1958

Beloved Ones of My Heart, today it is My Privilege in coming closer into outer physical conditions to release the Radiance of the Sacred Fire which My Love can bestow, and which My Love is to the Earth. I hope to make you aware of just how close We are to you sometimes, and how close We can always be to you when you give certain Obedience to the "Mighty I AM Presence" and to Us, in order to receive back into yourselves that which We can give you.

Now I would like you to make this experiment and notice how quickly after you make the Call and turn your attention to your "Beloved I AM Presence" first, and then to Us, how quickly there comes into your feeling world the Radiance, the Radiation of Our Love. I want you to realize it does not take thirty seconds for Our Love and Our Peace to come within your feeling world when you call to your

"Beloved I AM Presence" and to Us to make you feel
the Peace and the Flame of Love from Our Hearts.

Now if when you first do this a few times, you
only feel a stillness, try to realize that in that stillness
is Peace, and that Peace is Our Love. But don't allow
your intellect, because you have been quiet for a few
moments, to say to you, "Well, you made the Call
and you don't feel a thing!"

Once you make your Call to your "Beloved
I AM Presence" and to Us, stand with your Call and
be loyal to yourself. Don't allow the intellect or the
feeling to deny the Divine Command that you give! If
you will remember This, you will know what Instantaneous Manifestation means. The intellect and the
feeling have, for so long, been allowed to interfere
with the Love that is always flowing, the Love that is
always Peace, the Love that is always Purity, and that
is willing to give more of Itself than you could ever
use.

You must someday come to the time when you
master the outer self and never again permit it to interfere with the Peace and the Love from Our Great
Realms of Life which this World requires, which you
must have to attain your Mastery, and which is your
Protection against discordant conditions.

For I assure you, the Sacred Fire of Our Love,
the Peace of Our Love, is an Insulation and an

Armor of Protection about you when you understand that the moment you feel It, the Sacred Fire from Our Octave is flooding into you and around you to give you that which you require and to answer your Call.

Of course, Beloved Ones, We could draw Electronic Force in and around you that would shake you out of your seats, and it would be only Love that We would use. But to shock the outer self because it is rebellious is not Obedience to the Law, except when it becomes vicious. But what We want you to recognize, what We want you to do, is to *come into daily association with Us,* and you must *feel* Us and *feel* Our Love before you will see Us. Therefore when your love goes to your "Beloved I AM Presence" and then comes, for instance, to Me, and asks Me to fill you with the Peace and the Love of the Sacred Fire of My Heart, it would not take thirty seconds for you to begin to feel the Quiet, the Thrill, the Energy, the Power, and the Peace that I give instantly in answer to your Call.

We are closer to you than breathing and nearer than hands and feet. Therefore, if you will command the outer self to stand aside, and you ask Us to make you *feel* Our Outpouring of the Love and Peace of the Sacred Fire, I assure you We are perfectly capable of doing it, regardless of your human creation.

What do you think it is, sometimes, in the atmosphere of Earth, that suddenly stills everything? What do you suppose that is? It's a Wave of the Sacred Fire of Our Love, Our Purity, and Our Peace ·from Heights of Invincible Purity and Perfection. We can send that into the atmosphere of Earth, or in and around an individual as easily as you turn a flashlight upon something you're seeking, something you want to see. There is nowhere in the Universe that Our Sacred Fire Love cannot reach. There is nowhere that the Vibratory Action of Our Light and Its Peace cannot go, and there is nothing It cannot penetrate, because It is the Sacred Fire from the Heart of the Central Sun, and It is the All-Controlling Presence of everything, everywhere.

Therefore, if you want Peace within yourselves, then turn to your "Beloved I AM Presence" and to Me, and *demand the Sacred Fire Love and Peace of such Power in yourselves that you cannot help but feel It, and the Power that is so great It stills everything else around you.* We can turn This in and around you and let It surge for you, through you, and forward around you. We can let It flow to protect you. It can go before you and clear your way, and I assure you, It is All-Powerful.

Now, I want to give you a Secret today, that if you will master the outer self when it wants to be in turmoil, or turmoil is around you, if you will get in the habit of saying to everything in your emotional world: *"In the Name of the 'Mighty I AM Presence' and the Elohim of Peace, I command you, Peace, be still!"*

Say it with positive force, and then relax and begin to feel that Stillness—because I assure you, the continual turmoil and vibratory action of the emotional body is just like the ceaseless swinging of the waves on the ocean. There's a constant surge everywhere in the waters of the Planet. Your emotional bodies are made of the water element. Therefore, whatever disturbs the waters of the Planet will, to some degree, be felt by you unless you command your emotional body to feel otherwise.

If you will do this, sometimes when you have a desire to talk, where there is argument or turmoil, if you can command the outer self to be still until you can feel the Power of Our Peace and Love inside of you that holds control, then whatever it is necessary to say, you will say with Power, with Self Control; and you will find it effective, and you will find it makes you Victorious. If you do not do that and you speak under sudden excitement, you have no idea, sometimes, what rushes in and you have to handle weeks later. If you will prevent this—you just say, *"Peace, be still,"* until you feel that Peace from your "Presence" and the Love and Peace from Our Octave, as a rule it's scarcely one full minute till you will be so grateful that you did not speak, that you will begin to feel what the Power of the Silence is to control the turmoil in the feeling world of yourselves or those about you.

Now for your own enjoyment, I would like to try this experiment: When you want to *feel* and be absolutely certain that it is My Love and My Peace of the Sacred Fire coming into you and through you and around you, you can say to your "Mighty I AM Presence" and to Me, "*Thrill me with Your Peace! Thrill me with Your Peace! Thrill me with Your Peace, and hold control forever!*"

I will project under those conditions a certain Intensity of Electronic Force from Our Octave of Life, and a certain Action of the Sacred Fire from the Temple of Peace. As you become aware of This and feel It several times, many times when you are moving among conditions of the outer world and you least expect it, even when you're not thinking of Peace nor of Us, that Thrill will come in and around you, and that will be Our Electronic Force filling and surrounding you, giving you Protection and holding the Peace around you for your Victorious Accomplishment.

We want you to train yourselves to feel *Us,* and not the turmoil of the outer world; and that should be a very practical experience for you. *(applause)* Thank you so much.

Now, I have another very important reason for helping you to quiet the outer and feel Us at any moment in the midst of any condition. In the first place, as you set this habit, it will be very much easier for Us to direct you in the midst of outer conditions which might be in turmoil. But more than that, if you *demand that the Power, the Sacred Fire of Our Love and Peace comes into you, abides within, dwells within, and becomes you*—that means part of your Life Stream—there will come a tremendous Power and Majesty within you that will help you to Master every condition you contact in the outer world. It will be the calm, poised, humble control of Power that will go forth into conditions, prepare the way ahead of you, and make you successful always.

This will have a tremendous benefit upon your health; and more than that, It becomes the Magnet to draw to you by the very Peace which you hold within—It will draw to you the Blessings of the outer world which your Higher Mental Body wants to reach out and bring into your outer use to fulfill Its Great Divine Plan. This will affect your health. It will affect your finance. It will affect your business opportunity. It will affect everything you do in the outer life. There is no greater Power of Love and

Blessing that you can bestow by your Radiation than the Love of Our Peace, as Its Sacred Fire Presence enters into you and establishes in you and through and around you the Eternal Flame that comes from the Seven Mighty Elohim of Creation. This will enable many, many Blessings to come to you and within you when that Sacred Fire from Our Octave flows in and around you, and you love It and recognize It and know It has come within and around you to be part of your Life Stream, and you become Our Peace to Life wherever you abide.

These Magnificent Blessings and Powers of Life and Its Perfection are awaiting your use everywhere. We are the Custodians. We are the Givers of this Magnificent Sacred Fire to every Life Stream. Therefore, if you want the Intensification of any special Quality or Activity and you turn to your "Beloved I AM Presence" and to Us, I assure you the Cosmic Law is ready to pour the Sacred Fire's Love of any Quality into you the moment you ask—because you cannot ask for more Light or more Love or more Peace of the Sacred Fire without the Cosmic Law answering you instantly at your Call, for such ·is the Cosmic Law!

No matter what the experiences of the past have been, the moment you want more Light, more Love, and more Peace of the Sacred Fire to come and dwell within you, the Great Law of Life is such that It is given instantly into your outer use and direction. If you care to establish this habit, We will do everything to keep you close to Us, and to keep you enfolded in these Activities of the Sacred Fire that, I assure you, are all Love, all Light, and all Peace. Now, what could you ever have from That, that would ever give you anything of distress?

Do you not see that to turn to the Great Heart of Creation, your "Beloved I AM Presence" and the Ascended Masters and Cosmic Beings, and keep in close enough contact by your attention There—and your Heart's Desire will draw back to you the Limitless Blessings from Our Great Octave of Life. Since We are a Sun Presence that is always pouring Its Sacred Fire Love and Purity and Peace to Life, everywhere forever, you may have as intense a stream of that coming into yourselves as an Eternal Outpouring to your Life, just as intense as you desire.

If only mankind, more of the people of this World, understood who the Seven Mighty Elohim are and what Blessings you could have just for the asking, We could lift mankind very much more rapidly out of the discordant conditions that must be consumed.

So, if you will train yourselves to *feel* Me on the instant, the moment your love comes to your

"Mighty I AM Presence" and to Me, and you ask Me to make you *thrill* with My Sacred Fire Love of Peace, I assure you I can charge into you an Electronic Force that will be a *thrill* that will stay with you for days, and will always be with you whenever you recognize It! It takes your recognition, your acceptance, and your use of This in order to allow It to grow within you and expand Its Power, till Its Sun Presence in and around you controls all conditions and makes all things well.

Sometimes it's very difficult when We have these Magnificent Powers of Life, always ready to bless everyone and give only the Happiness of Perfection, to wait upon the waywardness of mankind– wait, and wait, and wait through century after century for individuals to wake up and reach up and desire the Blessings We can so easily give, and which bring such Happiness to Life, and are the Mastery of the Ascended Masters' Octave throughout creation.

So whenever the outer world weighs heavily upon you, or distress seems to swamp you or tries to touch you, if you can just go by yourself for a few moments and be still! *Ask your "Mighty I AM Presence" and Me to fill you and thrill you with the Sacred Fire of My Love and My Peace*. In just a moment everything within you will become still, and ease will come into your feelings; and as It continues, the *thrill* of that Power

becomes greater and greater, and the longer you let It
flow, the more Powerful It becomes. It can only
bring you the most Heavenly Joy and Power of Freedom.

I hope you feel the *thrill* that is within the room
this hour, for if I were to stay here and turn This on
you a little more strenuously, I would prove to you,
right now, the Fulfillment of My Words.

Many of you who were in the Chicago Class
when I first came, experienced This to which I have
reference. But now, I want you to open the Door and
invite into yourselves and into your affairs, the Sacred Fire Love and Peace from Our Great Realm of
Life, that Our Blessings and Our Power may fill your
world with Perfection and Victorious Accomplishment. We fill you with the Powers to fulfill and manifest the Divine Plan and close the door, by Our Love
and Our Peace, to that which has been the distress
and discord of the past.

You are at the crossroads of your life's experience. You have chosen to come thus far on the Pathway of Light; from now on it must be the Pathway of
Peace as you draw forth the greater Powers of your
"Beloved I AM Presence" or from the Assisting Masters, to enable you to accomplish greater things and
render the service to your Nation and your fellowman that you have the capacity to give, that is your

birthright, that is your obligation to your Country. We hope for the Sun Presence of your Peace to be an anchor within the Nation that prevents more destruction against your people.

I am not here by arbitrary cause. I am not come just to satisfy a few people in one place within this Nation. I am come to anchor into the structure of Earth itself here, and wherever the "I AM" Students abide, if they will make this Call, I can anchor like great Pillars of steel-like Force, the Power of Our Sacred Fire to hold Peace, to steady the Nation, to control the Powers of Nature, and to hold the Balance within this Land that enables the Divine Plan to be fulfilled, and Protection given to that which is constructive.

So, Beloved Ones, *I shall walk throughout the Nation today! (applause)* Thank you so much, Precious Ones.

I hope I may receive Calls enough to anchor Peace and Its Power within this Nation to hold control of it, and prevent the disturbance that is not Peace. Thank you so much; and won't you be seated, please.

If each of you will make this Call I have drawn to your attention, and then if you will *ask for the Cosmic Sun Presence of the Sacred Fire Love and Peace of the Seven Mighty Elohim to enter into the structure of your land and thrill the people with a force that compels them to hold Peace,* it will prevent many destructive things accomplishing their end.

So, Blessed Ones, as you enter into This and ask that Our Sacred Fire's Love and Peace *thrill* you within, and then the Sun Presence of Its Cosmic Action and Control *thrills* the Nation with the Power that holds Peace, you will give Us an opportunity to certainly reduce evil and—as the Sun Presence of Peace expands—prevent many, many things having to be handled by the people who will hold Peace under these conditions.

So, Blessed Ones, wherever you call forth the Sun Presence of Our Sacred Fire Love and Peace, demand Its Invincible Control and Limitless, Victorious Legions enter into the Nation now, and draw the Sacred Fire that is Their Dominion forever!

From Our Great Realm of Life all We can do is offer That which is the Sacred Fire's Perfection, and try to help individuals call It into outer action and use It to overwhelm the destructive forces, until they are forced to leave the Earth by the Action of the Cosmic Law.

Beloved Ones, this which I offer to you this hour is for the saving of the Nation; but as you recognize It and draw It within yourselves, you will find It the Healing Presence for yourselves individually.

Then It becomes the Controlling Force in the atmosphere about you, and It makes your pathway very much more comfortable.

As you go forward using this Sacred Fire, your own Mighty Powers will come into your outer use and give you Their Blessing and enable you to accomplish things that will bless Life everywhere. But if you care to call forth the Cosmic Pressure of Our Sacred Fire Love and Peace with such force that It *thrills* all wherever you direct It, some people will have some very interesting experiences. And even though they might seem not to feel It at the moment, as time goes on, I assure you they will; for I shall make It have Its effect within all Life, if a certain proportion of the people of this Land demand Its Cosmic Presence and Its Sacred Fire Control of that which exists within your borders.

Blessed Ones, I can come very close to you. I can give you Power that you have never used, and I can give you Assistance that will last forever.

So, if I am not intruding with My Presence, I assure you, I will be a Friend of Mighty Power whose Sacred Fire will enfold you and bless you forever, and lift you out of the limitations that you have experienced in the past. I hope to remain with you forever and fill the Nation that is the Heart of the World with the Peace of the Sacred Fire that should have been here and left here undisturbed. *(applause)* Thank you, Precious Ones.

Now, one more thought! If you *command everything you do to manifest Miracles of Eternal Peace and the Victory of Our Sacred Fire Love of the Seven Mighty Elohim,* just try it out and see for yourselves the change that will take place in your own surroundings, your own affairs. Then within you comes the Powerhouse from Our Octave that makes you ever more and more capable of producing Perfection here, controlling conditions, flooding the Limitless Blessings of the "Mighty I AM Presence" and the Ascended Host. And you, within the world of your own Sacred Fire's Love, become a Sun Presence that is the Healing Benediction of the World, and Peace has become a Reality for Eternity in you and all about you. Your Opportunities are Boundless, and your Blessings are without limit for Eternity.

May We all blaze as a Cosmic Sun Presence, the Sacred Fire Love and Peace of the Seven Mighty Elohim of Creation, and let It possess the Earth and all upon it, until Its Sun Presence raises all into the Ascension forever!

I shall never be farther away than your own Heart's Call; and My Opportunity to answer you, I hope will be continuous and without limit. May My Love prove what My Peace can do for you, and the

Sacred Fire enfold you and take Dominion of Its own. Thank you with all My Heart.

(Record CD 494)

Excerpts on the Elohim of Peace

Beloved Pelleur

When your attention was called to the Mighty
Elohim of Peace the day He came in Chicago–the
Saturday before last Christmas–the moment your
attention was turned to Him, you felt His Love come
back to you; and there was not a person sitting in that
room who did not feel It. He is a Cosmic Being of
Transcendent, Majestic Power–a Being who, with
one wave of His Hand, can cover the Earth with
Peace and still every vibratory action of everything
else. Whenever you have turned your attention to
Him, you have felt His Peace immediately, and have
been given ease and rest and happiness. He has answered your love through your attention.

("Voice of the I AM," November 1985)

Beloved Meru, God of the Andes

The Elohim of Peace and the Brothers of the
Golden Robe abiding upon the surface of the Earth of
the Three Americas, means the Expansion of the
Golden Flame within this portion of the World until
the permanent Golden Age has been outpictured in
the Americas, and the Radiation from That enfolds

the rest of the Earth to its Eternal Freedom. I convey
to you Their Love, Their Gratitude, and Their Blessings. Give Them Acceptance and Love; and call
Their Golden Flame into action to heal and to give
Peace to all. They are what you might call the Family of the Elohim of Peace. May you become His
Children also, and They, as your Elder Brothers,
show you Their Pathway of Peace through the
Golden Flame of Healing Love from Mighty Helios
and the Seven Mighty Elohim.

("Voice of the I AM," January 1979)

Beloved Elohim of Peace

. . . Visualizing the outer self enfolded in the
Sevenfold Flame of My Eternal Peace, feel that surrounded by a Sun, and wherever you move, move in
the Sun of that Flame, and you shall become the
Peace-Commanding Presence to the outer world
wherever you move, because as you hold the Picture,
I can intensify the Flame locally in and around you.
That becomes a Sun around you, growing greater
and greater, and the intensity of the Fire Element
within it becoming stronger and stronger as you use
It more. . . .

The Sevenfold Flame of My Eternal Peace is
Golden, the Heart Center is White, the outer radi-

ance Violet, turning into Blue at the outer edge. Now if you will hold this clearly, it will not take long for this to become permanently established around you in a Cosmic Action that will, many times, make individuals see that Flame about you. Many times you will see It yourself.

(Cassette SGC 5036)

CHAPTER VIII
Beloved Elohim of Peace

Chicago, Illinois
July 5, 1970

Beloved Ones of Our Heart, Beloved of the Light, Beloved of this Land of Freedom, We come tonight to anchor in and around you as much Love as possible, to protect you, to illumine you, to purify, heal, and raise everything in your being and worlds into the Heart Flame of Our Love, that everything of distress and limitation may be cut away, dissolved and consumed, and the Light of your own "Blessed Mighty I AM Presence" reveal Its Heart Love to the rest of the Universe.

I often want to do everything I can to remind the "I AM" Student Body of My Presence, because until you recognize that it is the Sacred Fire Love that changes conditions in the physical world permanently and constructively, until you will use this all the time—you have blessings from the outer world for a time, then you draw Our Sacred Fire Love for a time, then again the outer world takes your attention. And it goes back and forth, when you could just as well set

149

the habit and remember always as you call to your "Beloved I AM Presence," call to the Beloved Seven Mighty Elohim at the same time for Our Sevenfold Flame of Our Hearts' Love in and around your own Life Stream to blaze more Power into you and through you and around you, to give you Victory, to hold you harmonious, and to bring to you whatever you need from the outer world.

Now, Our Sacred Fire Love has a Twofold Action. We draw from the Great Central Sun and Our Temples of the Sacred Fire, the Sacred Fire Love into the brain structure through the Sevenfold Flame of the Seven Mighty Elohim; but We also have within that Love, the Power to see into the outer world and draw from the outer world into your outer use that which will assist your "Mighty I AM Presence" to fulfill Its Divine Plan within you as well as around you. So It is a Twofold Action from the Great Central Sun as well as through the constructive things in this World that We can bring into your outer use, as you remember Our Presence within you.

I think you don't quite understand what a Divine Being you are! I know you haven't thought so, and you do not think so of other Life Streams very frequently—once in a while. But you are really a Divine Being, because you have the Sacred Fire from the Heart of Creation within and around you, and

that is you; and We love you. So, We enfold you in
Our Heart Flame of Love from the Great Central Sun
to help you more quickly expand the Sacred Fire of
your own Heart's Flame, reveal Its Divine Plan, send
Its Blessing to the rest of the Universe, and use the
things in this World constructively, so you may have
more to use. As soon as you use everything constructively, your "Beloved I AM Presence" and the Seven
Mighty Elohim will always bring into your outer use
more and more of the constructive activities of the
physical world, to enable you to bless them and raise
them into greater and greater Light, until they, too,
become the Sacred Fire of Our Love.

This is a constant Raising Activity of the substance of the structure of the Earth, and the atmosphere, the waters of the Planet. It's a constant raising of everything in this World into the greater Purity
and Perfection of Our Sacred Fire Love.

Down through the centuries, in many civilizations and many nations of the World, mankind has
been shown a Crown or a Band around the head
with a Jewel in the front of the forehead. Well, this
represents the Light which We draw from the Great
Central Sun; this is the outer Symbol of Our Sacred
Fire, Our Heart Flame's Love within your brain
structure.

Mankind does not understand this; and therefore, the people do not give Us an opportunity to fill
the brain structure with Our Sacred Fire Love that
enables all the magnificent Creative Activities of your
"Mighty I AM Presence" and the Great Cosmic Beings to come into your outer use, to create magnificent things that are constructive and will be a Blessing
to all Life everywhere for Eternity.

Mankind needs to understand where the great
Treasure-house of the Universe is, what It contains,
what you can have in your outer use, and how necessary it is for you to expand It through yourselves.

This outer world has blest you tremendously,
Beloved Ones, century after century, as you have
embodied here again and again and again. You have
used the things of this World; you have used the substance and the Blessings of the Powers of Nature and
Forces of the Elements, and you have used many,
many, many things that the energy and consciousness
of other Life Streams have created in one civilization
after another. You have used these things that are the
gift of someone else's Life Stream. You have used
these many, many centuries down through the ages;
but you have not realized how much Life gives to the
use of the outer self when one embodies in the physical world.

Masses of mankind just take for granted everything in this World; and sometimes rebel furiously because the outer self doesn't have all it wants, when it has continually misused that which has been given in the past. We are the Eternal Protection, Almighty Cosmic Intelligence of the Great Central Sun's Sacred Fire Love, the Heart Flame of the Universe, the Heart Flame of Perfect Existence, the Heart Flame of one civilization after another, and the Heart Flame that enables you to attain the Ascension. No one can attain the Ascension without the Sacred Fire Love of the Seven Mighty Elohim, because when your "Mighty I AM Presence" and Higher Mental Body draw the Heart Flame within you up and into Itself, and into the Causal Body, We are the enfolding Sun Presence of Our Love that keeps everything still and untouched, until your Victory is attained.

We are constantly giving everything from the Heart of Creation into the outer use of mankind for the Fulfillment of the Great Divine Plan; and We will continue to give It. But there comes the time when, between embodiments, the outer self, if it has not served the constructive way of Life and has not fulfilled its own Divine Plan, the outer self must face the reaction of its own creation; and then We decide whether that Life Stream shall go on into more embodiments or whether that Life Stream must be withdrawn.

The "Mighty I AM Presence" and the Seven Mighty Elohim are the Deciding Authority and Power and Intelligence and Wisdom that says to the outer self—when it will not let Our Divine Plan be fulfilled, and that of the "Mighty I AM Presence"— We are the Ones who say: "Thus far and no farther can you have anything in this World. If you let not the Light expand through the Love that has blest you, then you must cease to be!" That outer intellectual consciousness is dissolved and consumed by the Sacred Fire of Our Love's Eternal Purity. Then the Higher Mental Body must try again and draw forth another Flame to establish another identity, an outer personal self. And again, We enfold that in Our Sevenfold Flame of the Seven Mighty Elohim.

So, there comes the time when there is the reckoning! Mankind cannot go on and consciously and constantly defy the greater Perfection of the Universe and the Intelligence that creates It and the Love that gives It. The outer intellectual consciousness and the outer feeling cannot go on indefinitely and defy the Perfection of Love that is so Great that It fills Infinite Space with Magnificent Miracle Manifestations. The outer self that defies That must of necessity realize there comes the moment when either you are grateful to Life or you must cease to be.

This is the Peace which We bring when mankind turns to the Light lovingly, willingly, gratefully, and understands Life enough to cooperate with It, so the outer self may be comfortable, produce Perfection, reach Mastery, and become a Co-creator with Us in the atmosphere of this World and all Worlds to come.

Our Love is not to be sneered at, and transgressed, and ignored, and ridiculed, and defied, and refused, without penalty! When Life is so magnificent, and Life gives so constantly to produce the manifestation of Perfection to bless all Infinity, mankind cannot go on and defy the Law of My Peace, the Law of My Harmony, the Law of My Love, without terrific suffering.

Mankind needs to awaken and develop gratitude and understanding that the Infinite Universe is Master over the finite, and Our Infinite Love of the Seven Mighty Elohim of Creation, Our Sacred Fire Hearts' Flame is Master over the selfishness of mankind, the filth and the destruction of human creation— and is Master over the Powers of Nature and Forces of the Elements, all of which have blest the outer personal self in one embodiment after the other.

Now I come to you today to expand through you, if you will let Me by remembering Me, to expand through your own consciousness, your brain structure, your outer mind, your outer intellectual consciousness; and to expand through the energy of your feeling world My Heart Flame's Love, the Love that gives the Peace that surpasseth the understanding of the mind. I come to give the Love that sets all Free, purifies all things, perfects all things, and raises all into greater and greater Perfection of that Love.

If mankind will remember Me, and let My Heart Flame's Love fill the outer self with what I know keeps out the destructive forces of the outer world, I can be the Invincible Protection within your feeling world of the energy of your own Life Stream, to keep the destructive forces of the outer world from pressing heavily upon you, or imposing their destructive qualities that sometimes you have not realized are surrounding you and are responsible for much failure, destruction, and desecration.

"I AM" Master of everything in the Universe by the Love and the Purity and the Peace which "I AM", and That is Power without limit. That is the Concentration of Energy that has become the Sacred Fire that nothing in this World can ever change. Nothing!

I wish to explain Our Blessings and Our Service to Life, Our Divine Plan's Fulfillment, and Our Effort to assist the Mighty Saint Germain to purify and save this Nation that is the Heart of the World. And if We do not save it, you will not have civilization anywhere in the World! You will not have beings taking embodiment in this World unless this Nation is purified and protected and saved, that its Heart may hold Our Love to help the rest of the World go forward to its Ascension.

Mankind needs to understand the Heart Flame of Life from which Perfection always comes, which is Eternal, which is forever expanding, and which is the Victory and the Ever-illumining Presence of the Ascended Masters' Octave of Perfection.

Mankind can have Limitless Love and Purity, and Power without limit to wipe out everything in this World that is less than Perfection, if mankind wants It. If mankind will look up to That which is greater than itself, and ask for the greater Perfection, and then realize that the outer self must be purified if it is going to be worthy to use that greater Perfection which the outer self many times wants, but will not make the outer self worthy of Its Presence.

You must be worthy of Life's Great Blessings, Precious Ones. When mankind misuses the Divinest Gifts in all Infinite Space, the Divinest Powers of Life's Perfection—mankind is entrusted with those Blessings, those Powers of Creation, then certainly

They carry a Responsibility to the individual who is blest by those Activities of Life within the outer personal self.

I shall develop Gratitude and Understanding, Reverence and Peace within the feeling of the outer self of every individual to whom I give My Love, because there must come Honor, and Reverence, and Adoration, and Conscious Illumination and Understanding of That which is greater than mankind. Mankind must understand the greater Perfection and Blessing that Love alone can manifest; and down here, mankind must make itself worthy of that Love if human beings' discord and limitations and destruction are to be consumed.

The Great Cosmic Law which is embodied in the Great Cosmic Beings who have created this Earth and this System of Worlds—if They have placed in this World the Magnificent Life of the Powers of Nature and Forces of the Elements, and the Love of Their own Life Streams, to provide a Planet upon which mankind can embody and draw forth the Master Powers of Life to attain the Ascension, and become a Creator of a World or a System of Worlds like those Cosmic Beings, if mankind does not awaken to its responsibility to the Universe around it, and understand that the constructive way of Life is the only right way to live, and remember the Honor and the Reverence that is due to That which is greater than itself, if mankind will not learn that lesson, then there must come the suffering of the human creation charged back into the creator of its frightful misuse of Life.

Life is very Wonderful, Beloved Ones! Life Itself, from the Great Central Sun, is the container of everything that is of Perfection. All the Intelligence of Infinite Space is within Life. All the magnificent Substance and Energy and Consciousness that creates Worlds and Systems of Worlds is all within Life, and Life is the only thing you have to use to produce any kind of manifestation.

Therefore, mankind must awaken to some kind of Love and Gratitude and Understanding of the Responsibility of using Life! Life is the Divine, Immortal Existence of the Great Central Sun; and when the outer personal self of human beings in this World continually uses the Blessings of the Powers of Nature and Forces of the Elements, and continually misuses them, then there must come Conscious Understanding that the Infinite Universe around this physical World is the Infinite Life of Infinite Perfection and Infinite Power and Infinite Intelligence, much greater than all mankind put together. This will come! *(applause)* Thank you so much. Won't you be seated, please.

Mankind has pushed aside and turned its back upon the Infinite Intelligence of Perfection when the outer self becomes discordant; and *there is only one thing in all Eternity can open the Door for the Infinite Perfection of Life to come back into the use of a Life Stream that has turned away from the Light—only one thing can bring the Light that turns the individual back to the Perfection from whence it came and from whence comes all that is Good,* and the only Source there is of Peace and Happiness and Purity and Perfection and Victory.

Mankind must be purified; but those of the Life Streams in this World who are turning to the Light at this time and trying to call to God as they understand it, many of them have very, very great Light in the Causal Body, which means that they have the Power to arise and accomplish the Ascension if a certain amount of Help is given from Our Ascended Master Octave. *That is why the Mighty Saint Germain brought the use of the Violet Consuming Flame, so as many Life Streams as possible could turn to the Light at this time, understand Our Existence, accept Our Love, and use It to purify the outer self, and to help purify the Nation and help Us purify the World.* This is the only Release from mankind's distress. It's the only Release there is from mankind's frightful, destructive human creation. It's the only release that can ever come to take mankind out of war, and take war off of the Earth.

Mankind must learn to be reverent to that Infinite Universe by which it is surrounded, that blesses it constantly with the greater Life and the greater Light that is the Love from the Great Central Sun, that illumines the Earth and sustains your life every day.

If the Physical Sun and Its Light and Its Love were withdrawn, you could not exist in this World. Mankind must understand something beside its own discord; and the Fullness of everything that is the Ascended Masters' Perfection of Eternity is contained within the Sevenfold Flame of the Heart Flames of the Seven Mighty Elohim of Creation.

We are the Guardians of the Cosmic Powers that created this Planet and brought the Powers of Nature upon it for mankind's use. We are the Builders of Creation! We are the Guardians of the Heart Flame from the Great Central Sun; and there must come some kind of Conscious Understanding of the Reality of Our Existence, and the Purity that is imperative if mankind is to understand the Truth of Existence and cooperate with the great Powers of Mastery that can be drawn here to raise all into the Ascension.

Everything that you want to fulfill the Divine Plan or do anything that is constructive, depends on the Harmony and the Purity of Our Love! It de-

pends on the Harmony and Purity of the Love of
your "Mighty I AM Presence"! It depends on the
Harmony and the Purity and the Love of the Physical Sun. Then it's time mankind understood that the
Divine Beings, who are that Almighty Perfection of
Life, are the Authority over this World—and not
mankind's destruction.

This is what We want to bring to your consciousness; and if you will hold the Sevenfold Flame
of the Seven Mighty Elohim within and around your
own forehead, the Heart within It, and you will hold
This around everyone that you contact, if you'll just
form the habit of seeing that Light, that Flame expand
around the brain structure, you will shut off a great
deal of the misconcepts from within the consciousness
of the Life Streams for which you do that. You will
disconnect any of those Life Streams from their suggestions coming to you, if you will wear the same
Crown of the Sacred Fire of Our Love, the Sacred
Fire of the Seven Mighty Elohim's Love, which understands everything in infinite space, knows all the
past, all the future, all that is of the present.

Now I bring This to you, and ask you to establish the habit of holding This upon your own forehead and also around those you contact, because
This is what is represented by the Crowns of rulers of
the centuries past in the various nations of the World.

The Crown has always represented the Ascended Masters' Control of the Consciousness of the Life Stream that wears the Crown. And when the Sacred Fire of Our Love is the Jewel that holds within the brain structure the Protecting Love and Purity and Presence that allows the "Mighty I AM Presence" to hold Perfection in outer world conditions, then there comes into outer physical conditions the Perfection from Our Octave. And I can assure you, you may try everything in this world that's in existence now in the outer world, and you will never have Perfection without the Assistance of the Seven Mighty Elohim's Sevenfold Flame in your own consciousness—your own outer intellectual consciousness and the outer intellectual consciousness of everyone with whom you have to deal.

If people would only understand This and hold the Picture, and understand what it means to use the Sacred Fire Love of Consciousness, whether it be within the individual or other individuals, We could blaze Perfection without limit for all Eternity. Every human being on Earth has the Sacred Fire of Our Hearts' Love within the brain structure.

Now, if you will form the habit of calling the Illumining Love of the Seven Mighty Elohim of Creation, as well as your "Mighty I AM Presence," which you call to first, if you will *call the Illumining Love and*

Fiery Christ Truth of the Seven Mighty Elohim of Creation into everything you do, and realize that you have a right to use the Sacred Fire of Our Life to help you do what you want to do in the physical world to produce Perfection, sustain it, and expand it for all Eternity, We can open the Door and perform such Miracles through you as you cannot comprehend until you begin to use the Power and have the Miracle Manifestations in your outer use that come only from Our Love. *(applause)* Thank you so much.

Now, ordinarily your intellect thinks that it's your own thought that is doing something down here. You have to think something, and then you try out here to do something to fulfill what you desire to do. But when you begin to recognize that it's the Heart Flame of your "Mighty I AM Presence" that contains all Perfection and is the Treasure-house of your Life Stream, and the Heart Flame of the Seven Mighty Elohim is the Sacred Fire Treasure-house and Love and Perfection from the Great Central Sun that has been given in and around you to protect the Treasure-house of your "Mighty I AM Presence," you will begin to realize that no matter what you want to do, you are using the Sacred Fire of Our Life to help you do it.

You are using the Sacred Fire of the Life of your "Mighty I AM Presence" whenever you produce something constructive; whenever you produce Perfection, you are using the Sacred Fire of Our Life. But when you use just the outer intellectual consciousness, which is the energy and the suggestions of the world around you, you make mistakes, you have limitations, you have problems, you have disaster, you have suffering, you have everything that you don't want.

So, from this hour I hope you will remember to control your life, and want to control everything within you by the Sacred Fire Love of your "Mighty I AM Presence'" Heart Flame, and the Sacred Fire Love of the Seven Mighty Elohim of Creation to be Our Victory, Our Life's Control within you, that at all times gives you the Power to do out here in the physical world whatever your service is, and do it always perfectly, hold Protection around what you do, and at all times maintain Harmony, because Our Sacred Fire Love cannot produce discord. You cannot misuse It. You cannot requalify It. You cannot produce anything but Perfection when you use Our Ascended Master Life, which Our Heart Flame's Love is. And I am quite sure your "Mighty I AM Presence" will appreciate very, very greatly if you do not experiment any longer with the mistakes of the outer world. *(applause)* Thank you so much.

Now, if you experiment with Our World, you can't have mistakes because Our World doesn't contain any! If you use Our Heart Flame's Purity, Love, and Peace in anything you do, there cannot come within you anything but Our Perfection. And if you would always say to your "Blessed Mighty I AM Presence": *"Fill me and let me accomplish everything by Your own Heart Flame's Indestructible, Invincible Purity, Love, and Peace,"* you couldn't create discord in yourselves or in outer world conditions. So this is simply a matter of drawing in and around yourselves that which We know produces Perfection for Eternity. Then you become like the Sun, a Radiating Presence of Our Heart Flame's Love, a Radiating Presence of the Sacred Fire Love of your own "Mighty I AM Presence."

Then the Angelic Host can accompany you, can draw more Sacred Fire around you and control outer physical world conditions for your Protection, your Prosperity, your Healing, and clothe you with the Power to help the rest of Life rise out of the self-created shadows of mistakes and suffering and limitation and death—because the second death only comes when mankind will not turn back and use the Sacred Fire of Our Love to do what needs to be done inside the physical body and into the outer world conditions, and let Harmony and Purity and Love set

things into Divine Order, purify things, set all into
Divine Order, hold Perfect Balance, which is Divine
Justice—and let the Divine Plan of the Ascended Masters' Octave be drawn into the physical conditions of
this World, create the Peace of Eternity, and the Illumination that forever expands Its greater and
greater Blessings and Treasure-house of existence.

Blessed, Blessed, Blessed Ones, when We have
furnished the Heart Flames of Our Love into the
physical bodies of mankind—millions and millions
and billions, century after century after century—don't
you think sometime We want you to awaken, and all
mankind awaken, realize the Reality of Our Presence,
and understand what We can do to set mankind Free
from its own darkness, its own distress, and its own
misunderstanding of Life, until the continual Purification takes place that returns the outer intellectual consciousness into the use of the Higher Mental Body.

Your outer consciousness can just as well be
filled with the Light and the Perfection and the Victory of the Higher Mental Body, as to let your intellect accept the things of the outer world that are not
the Perfection of Life. And if you ask the Seven
Mighty Elohim to charge you with Their Ascended
Master Consciousness of what We know will make
you Master over the discord of the World, you'll
open the Door and give Us an Opportunity to fill you

with Our Life's Love, Our Purity, Our Perfection, and Our Light, that can tell you ahead of time whether a thing is going to be a success or not.

Your need is to blaze Light into the future, and you need it to close the door of the past against the remembrance of the discord and the distress and the destruction and the failure of the mistakes of the past. Please don't remember anything that is a mistake of the past! Don't let the outer world's intellectual explanation say, "Well, you have to learn from the mistakes of the past." You don't have to do anything of the kind! You make God dependent on evil if you say that. Don't accept it!

You can have all the Sacred Fire Illumining Love and Intelligence and Almighty Perfection of Eternity to come right into you, and tell you the Perfection that is needed for you to hold control of outer physical conditions, and that forever makes you master of circumstance. We ask you to do this because We want to close the door of the past; We want to help you plan the Perfection of the future, but you never live any time but this immediate second! Your *Eternal Now* is the only time you can ever live—the *Eternal Now*, this immediate instant! The past is gone, the next one has not come yet; so you can only live in the *Eternal Now*.

This is what We want you to fill with the Heart Flame of your own "Mighty I AM Presence'" Divine Plan fulfilled every instant for you—fill the outer self with Our Heart Flame's Perfection of Our Purity, Our Love, Our Peace, Our Perfection and Mastery of Eternity that none can ever change, that your distress may cease, you may express your Mastery, you may draw forth Cosmic Powers to help your fellowman, and to help free your Nation from that which otherwise will destroy and desecrate everything.

Blessed Ones, We simply beg you to live by Our Sacred Fire Hearts' Flame, that you may forever be at Peace. That is why I am the Elohim of Peace, because My Love is Indestructible Peace, Indestructible Power without limit, Indestructible Illumination, Indestructible Wisdom, and Indestructible Control of all Manifestation.

So when conditions battle you and are the limitations of the outer, stop a moment and call forth the Heart Flame of your "Mighty I AM Presence," and the Heart Flames of the Seven Mighty Elohim, to fill you with what We know makes you Victorious over the conditions of the outer world that are trying to battle you when you want to do something constructive.

I trust We will be able to help you be victorious in anything and everything constructive that

you attempt to do, and you will not have to be de-
layed in the accomplishment of something that is
worth doing and does fulfill the Divine Plan that
helps the rest of mankind to be Free. We want you
to be that Victory now. *(applause)* Thank you so
much.

Now I'll give you one more thought, one more
effort. When you say to your "Beloved Mighty I AM
Presence," at night before you go to sleep and when
you awaken in the morning: *"'Beloved Mighty I AM
Presence' and the Seven Mighty Elohim, make me the Victory
of Your own Hearts' Flame in everything I do, and prevent all
else forever,"* you can't make a mistake! You can't help
but be constructive! You can't help but have the Perfection which Our Love is, and It will close the door
to anything of uncertainty in the future. It will make
you master of circumstance; and when you become
My Heart's Flame of All-Purifying Love and Peace,
and you hold That within yourselves, you become
the Controlling Manifestation by the Sacred Fire of
Our Octave over conditions in which you must live,
and which will serve you only in the constructive
way of Life.

My Heart's Flame Way to live Life is Peace;
and there isn't anything else can come within the
Flame of My Victory over everything in Creation!
Thus We come to the place where you can help Us

purify the Nation and the World by purifying people and conditions wherever you pass by or with which you have to deal.

So, don't be a part any longer of the distress and the destruction and the desecration and the uncertainty and the fear of outer world conditions, when We can flash the Flame of Our Hearts' Love and place It anywhere in outer world conditions if you will call It forth. And It is as free as the air you breathe! It is the Mastery and the Perfection from the Heart of Creation. It is the Almighty Partnership of your own "Blessed Mighty I AM Presence" from the Great Central Sun; and We will forever send Legions of the Angels of Our Love to hold Its Flame in and around you whenever you want Them, whenever conditions around you are to have to be protected, and are to be sustained to fulfill the Divine Plan that raises the rest of Life into Our Purity and Our Perfection in the Victory of the Ascension. And there is no Eternal Peace without Our Flame of Purity and Love and Mastery over all in this World.

So, We come and will forever watch every opportunity to plant, as it were, Our Hearts' Flame through your Calls into outer physical world conditions, until they have become purified enough to be the revealment of the Ascended Masters' Divine Plan fulfilled that purifies this World and raises mankind into Our World of Perfection for Eternity. And this is the Victory that lies ahead of you. It is the Way and Means harmoniously provided that produces only Mastery and Perfection, and is forever the only Freedom in Existence.

This is what your Mighty Saint Germain brought to you when He offered you the use of the Violet Consuming Flame, because the Sevenfold Flame of the Violet Consuming Flame is anchored within your brain structure, and This must be drawn into physical conditions for Purification.

Therefore, We offer Our Hearts' Sacred Fire Love's Indestructible Mastery and Victory over everything you can ever contact, and We want to fill you with Our Hearts' Love first, that you may be the Almighty Sun Presence of Our Love in this World, that pours to the rest of Life whatever brings Illumination and returns mankind to the Ascended Masters' Control of conditions in this World, until the Peace for which mankind calls has become the Purity and the Love of everyone's Life in this World for Eternity, and there is no other Divine Plan to be fulfilled.

So Peace is necessary for your survival, and Our Sacred Fire Hearts' Flame and Love are that Peace; and that Peace is necessary for you to survive to fulfill the Divine Plan. It is necessary through you for your Nation to survive, and it's necessary through the Nation for the World to be purified and returned to the constructive way of Life.

So, if you will remember Us, We will remember you; and may the Fullness of all the Victory which Our Purifying Love and Peace are to Life reveal through you the Mastery that forever brings Freedom to the Earth and the Ascension to all mankind forever.

Thank you with all My Heart.

(Record CD 1630)

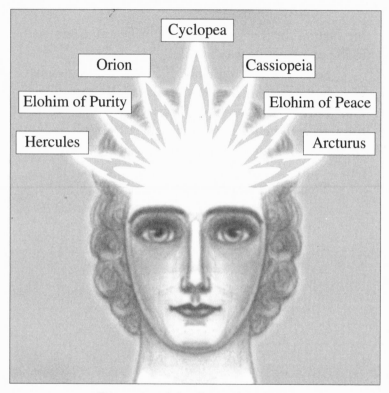

Diagram of the Sevenfold Flame

In visualizing the Sevenfold Flame within your own forehead, Beloved Arcturus' Flame is located on the left side of your forehead and Beloved Hercules' Flame is on the right side of your forehead, as depicted in the illustration.

CHAPTER IX
Beloved Elohim of Purity
To the "I AM" Ascended Master Youth

Chicago, Illinois
January 2, 1950

Beloved "I AM" Ascended Master Youth of the Mighty Saint Germain, and of Light everywhere, We come to you today, bringing the Joy and the Enjoyment of Our Great Powers of Life's Perfection, all of which you crave within yourselves, sometimes knowingly and sometimes unknowingly. Sometimes the desire for Our Purity and Perfection is a craving within your feeling world that never is satisfied until you receive That which We alone can give. And if you will learn to Charge the outer self with the Satisfaction of Our Great Love and Purity to Life, you will not be touched by the conditions of the outer world that are purely hypnotic—because anything and everything that is not the Eternal Perfection of Life and Its Mighty, Great, Infinite Love from the Great Central Sun, all that is not Our Eternal Purity, all that is not the Limitless Freedom and Unconditional Use of all Life's Powers of Perfection, everything that is not That, is of the sinister force and is nothing but hypnotic suggestion.

Now, We want to take you through the experiences that are still ahead of you, untouched by those conditions of the outer world that strike into the average person.   Because they do not know how—individuals of the outer world do not know how—to shut that out, they go down under its failure. I want you to feel today that if you want the Master Powers of Life—which We have the Authority to confer upon you so long as you place your "Mighty I AM Presence" first and send It your love, and then call to Us for whatever added Powers are required to enable your Life Stream to take you forward victoriously in anything to which you turn your attention, so long as it be constructive—We will clothe you with Power without limit to accomplish everything your Hearts desire!

Now, We are trying to clothe you in Mantles of Our Substance and those Activities of the Sacred Fire that will take you through outer world conditions. While you may observe them and see the effects they produce, yet you will be kept free from the desire to enter into that which would one day wreck you.

The great Law of Purity is the Law of Perfection, and since all Powers of the Universe are held within that great Treasure-house of Life's Mighty

Cosmic Christ Love, then if you simply demand that the outer self become a Blazing Sun of Its Presence, and the Violet Consuming Flame consumes all else, then as you demand your Invincible Protection, you are armored with a Strength of the Light and Our Purity that makes it safe for you to use these greater Powers of Life, and thus, you make yourselves worthy of Their use in the physical world; and someone must draw Them into outer use, My Dear Ones, if there is to be any improvement among mankind.

You might think mankind are progressing by this, that, or the other outer world accomplishment; but I tell you, until the people return to Purity, there is no permanent improvement! They might want Purity, and they might rebel furiously against the penalty that they are constantly paying for impurity; but unless they will turn in humble, grateful obedience to that "Mighty I AM Presence" and clothe themselves in Its Eternal, Invincible Love of Eternal Purity, unless That comes first, they will but go on marking time, doing and undoing the things they desire to do in the outer world. Mankind have gone on for two and a half million years, building, building, building—and tearing down what they have built.

What do you think abides today on the Earth in the way of constructive accomplishment, which has been saved, or carried through the centuries of the

past, that is now to come into the outer use of those
who are to build the Permanent Perfection of the future? Everything that is of value on this Earth that
has been a constructive accomplishment of the past,
all that has been preserved in the beds of the oceans,
hermetically sealed, all that has been preserved in the
Retreats, all that is of any permanent existence on the
Earth has been preserved and protected by the Ascended Host, not by mankind themselves.

So, if you want Protection in the future, if you
want to be assured of your victorious accomplishment, no matter what you want to do so long as it be
constructive, then you must have Our Invincible,
Eternal Purity and Our Protection about you, both
while you are doing it and about the ways and means
that you are going to use; and if you don't have that
Protection, well then, some destructive force moves in
just about the time you think you are going to reach
for your Victory; some destructive force moves in
and takes it out of your hands. Then you feel very
resentful because you didn't attain the success you
desired.

Now you are the builders of the future! You
have to carry the responsibilities of the conditions of
this Nation in the future, and almost in the present—in
the not-far-distant future. But unless you are armored, My Dear Ones, in Our Eternal, Invincible

Purity, unless you call forth the Cosmic Christ Love through your "Mighty I AM Presence," and unless you demand Invincible Protection around yourselves and around that which you are going to accomplish, you will find yourselves interrupted intermittently, or interfered with from time to time, in everything you undertake until you gain the Strength and the Power to move into outer action that Force of the Sacred Fire that mows down everything that dares to oppose God and God's Perfection of that "Mighty I AM Presence."

You might just as well make up your minds now to move into action with your concentrated attention upon this "Presence," demand these Powers of Invincible Victory into yourselves, because Victory is not attained just by your Decrees and making your Calls. Victory is attained by the Obedience of the outer self unto the Great Currents of Energy released by the "Presence" and Ourselves, which have to flow through you to do the things that fulfill the Divine Plan.

So, you must take yourselves in hand first, and demand the Invincible Purity that is Eternal Strength, because without Purity you don't have Eternal Strength; and if, sometimes, you feel rather weary and weighted down, you are weighted down by the impurity of the outer world. And therefore, if you arise in the Strength and Courage and Power of your own Heart's Flame of the "Mighty I AM Presence" and demand the Cosmic Christ Love from the Great Central Sun come through your "Presence" into you, come into your affairs and stand your guard, and then you call to Us for whatever Powers it is Our Privilege to direct into your use, you will strengthen yourselves before you use the Power.

Now, because of the hypnotic suggestions of the outer world, and it is a trick of the sinister force as old as the sinister force itself—is to get the individual to dash into something without sufficient preparation, and thereby either produce failure or unnecessary struggle, or warp the ideas so that Perfection cannot come through.

You are the builders of the future! You can build the Mightiest Perfection that has ever come to this Earth, if you want to. This group of "I AM" Students alone, you of the Youth, the "I AM" Ascended Master Youth of the World, if there were no more of you to go forward in this Service to America than is right here in this room, if you understand Me today and will take your Stand before you start anything, that you *demand the Mightiest Cosmic Christ Love of all Eternity come through your "Presence" and into the outer self, and enter here, and you demand Its Victory in you, and then you demand that We clothe you in that Great Cosmic Sa-*

cred Fire of Our Eternal, Invincible Purity and Powers from the Ascended Masters' Octave, that enables you to go forth and do these things with the great Joy and Love that Life intends— you will never know struggle, you will never know lack, you will never know limitation or interference or delay!

I think it is well worth everything that it takes in your individual effort to clear your pathway ahead, so that when you start to accomplish something you have one Victory after another. You go forth to Attainment to bring forth This! You bless It. You protect It. Command It to expand, and you then take the next greater responsibility and fulfill the Divine Plan concerning It. That way you go on from one Magnificent Accomplishment to another in the Greatest Joy mankind has ever known.

I want to take out of your lives all sense of struggle and trouble. Trouble cannot abide where Our Love is; trouble cannot be where Our Purity and Its Mighty Flame move into outer action; and it is but energy, Precious Ones. All of the energy that seems to be opposition in your worlds is nothing but energy vibrating at a slow rate, while if you charge it with Our Eternal, Invincible Purity, you step up its frequency, you charge it with Our Happiness, and It thrills you and energizes you and protects you, and lifts you to that exhilaration of Magnificent Accomplishment, and you never know failure. Now please, accept This today; and don't let any human being on this Earth discourage you, or imagine God created them as a special authority to dominate you.

Now I do not mean to defy your parents, not at all! They have given you a tremendous blessing, they have given you the body in which you are to attain your Ascension. They are worthy of your honor, your love, your assistance, your obedience. But if you call the Mighty Christ Love, the Mightiest of all Infinity from the Great Central Sun through your "I AM Presence" into the outer self, and this Power radiates through you, It will clear your way! It will dissolve your problems! It will be the Light in the darkness; and It will be the Strength to you to go forward, and dare to do and enjoy your Victory over the forces of this World.

Why, you might just as well have your Victory with enjoyment as with a sense of struggle. Correcting conditions of the Earth is no long-faced process to Us, I'll assure you. When We enjoy the great Music of the Spheres, and We choose to draw that Power into a Flame and spread It over mankind's discord, what can the discord do? It has to dissolve and disappear, and so it is with you.

We want to keep turning your attention back to your "Mighty I AM Presence," and the necessity for drawing the Mightiest Cosmic Christ Love in the Universe, which means the Love, those Activities of the Sacred Fire from the "Mighty I AM Presence" in the Great Central Sun—with which your Life Stream was *One* in the beginning. You always have been, and you always will be; but you had certain Activities of Life in the Great Central Sun which are still held in Trust for you by your Higher Mental Body and by your "Electronic Presence"; and you may have that Inheritance, you may have any Faculty that is within Life that produces Perfection into your outer use by the attention of your intellect, and the love of your Heart.

There is nothing too great to accomplish! There is nothing too small to be worthy of your Command and Attention of Perfection; and there is no obstacle, My Dear Ones, for those who face that "Presence." And I don't mean in a just half-hearted way, or in some terrific fear when problems seem to be terribly pressing upon you. I mean to make it a daily, hourly, momentary habit of the outer self: Just pour wave after wave of love to the "Mighty I AM Presence"! Thank It for everything. Accept that the next Wave is infinitely greater. Go forth and use It to beautify the world, purify it, and lift all you contact. Use It to give Courage and Strength and Illumination to the rest of mankind. Use It to purify conditions of the outer world. Thank the "Presence"; pour It back, and receive the next wave greater.

Now, it's as easy and it's as mechanical as the turning up of your volume control on your broadcasting or radio sets. It doesn't make any difference what it is; you are using energy. You may draw as much as you want, or as little. Your Free Will determines what you want in the outer; but so long as persons, places, conditions, or things make you think that you have to accept their discord and their imperfection, well then, just so long will that be a pressure around you, until you arise and shatter the whole thing, and *demand the Victory of Cosmic Christ Love charge you with Its Ever-expanding Endless Power and Strength and Courage to go forward and flash the Flame of Perfection, and command It manifest in the physical octave.* And then sustain and expand It, until wherever you move mankind will realize you have the Power to produce Perfection, and you are about your Father's Business when you enjoy bringing It into the outer use.

There is a great Law of Energy and Vibration which you have been told of, need to be reminded of again and again. The great Cosmic Law of Energy, which is Life, is not stingy; but It does not permit any unnecessary use of Itself. Therefore, if there is an unnecessary use of the energy or the substance or the supply of your world, it's going to come back some day as a shortage. Now then, supposing these mistakes have been made; supposing there are these limitations in the appearance world—you can take every one of them as they come to you, and *demand that the Hand of the "Mighty I AM Presence" strike Its Cosmic Sword of Blue Flame into the condition, burn it up instantly, compel the annihilation of its cause and all intended through it; and then demand the Unfed Flame in Its Cosmic Christ Action of the Mightiest Love of all Creation come there to abide forever!*

Then, wherever you move, you will replace imperfection with the Flame of Perfection; and you cannot go on and flood This into the atmosphere around you constantly as a matter of habit, without yourselves automatically becoming That. Now this is simply the Law of Energy and Vibration. It is no respecter of persons. It doesn't know who you are, doesn't know anything about your motive, doesn't know what you are going to do with the energy. If you call for energy, energy comes and is released. If you qualify it with limitation and discord, or domination over someone else, it's going to come back and dominate you.

If there is shortage of anything in your world, know that it has a cause, My Dear Ones! It couldn't be in your world, or in touch with your world, or contact your world, if it weren't somewhere originally connected with the energy of your world. And therefore, if it is connected—supposing it is a return of something that is a mistake of the past, say, *"All right, since you're my Life and I have done this thing to you, I now lift you by the Love and Forgiveness of the Cosmic Christ, that Life of mine in the Great Central Sun whose Violet Consuming Flame draws you into the Heart of Its Love, purifies you, consumes everything that is of discord, clothes you with the Unfed Flame, and you go forward now as my Freedom!"*

My Dear Ones, you can take every problem, every bill, every limitation that you have, whether it be mind, body, or affairs, and by that use of the Violet Consuming Flame and your Call to the Cosmic Christ Love, the Mightiest of all Eternity, to move into action, into those things, and pouring that Love upon that, command that energy to become the Authority of your Freedom; and manifestations and conditions of Freedom will appear, as surely as you do it, as surely as you exist in the Universe today. And no matter, Precious Ones, how great this activity becomes, no matter how wonderful your accomplishment is, please remember My Words today: *remain humble, and grateful, and obedient to that "Mighty I AM Presence," and give It full credit for everything!*

As your Power becomes great, Precious Ones, the sinister force has many subtle ways of touching you, whereby it would throw you into some other channel where sooner or later discord would manifest; and you do not need to experience those conditions. The greater your Power becomes, the more humble and unselfish should be your attitude to your "Mighty I AM Presence" and the Ascended Host, because They have given you all! Anything good in your world today is the Gift of that "Mighty I AM Presence" and the Ascended Host; and anything that is not Their Freedom, and Their Love and Happiness and Power, is but the misqualification of your own thoughts and feelings of the past.

Now I want you to be cut free today! You, as the "I AM" Ascended Master Youth, should become the Authority of Freedom, My Dear Ones. After all, Beloved Saint Germain has made you a Part of His own Family; and as the Messenger gave you the Explanation before the Dictation began, when He has drawn you as a Part of Himself into His Great Activity and Authority, mark you, to command Freedom to the Earth, then you can have all the Ways and Means of producing Freedom for yourselves and for others.

You can be the Courage of His Freedom! You can be the Authority of His Freedom to use the Violet Consuming Flame without reservation, and compel every condition of discord to be turned upside-down and become a Miracle of Love and Blessing to you. Then nothing will disturb you. You will travel on an even plane; for that Cosmic Love of the Mighty Christ Presence, the "Mighty I AM" and the Great Central Sun holds Eternal Command. And your Invincible Purity, My Dear Ones, within your own inner secret thoughts and feelings will be outpictured and answered by the greater Purity in your affairs that produces Perfection that fulfills the Law.

Now remember, there is an old statement you have heard many, many times: "You think in secret, and you feel in secret" (so you think), "and the Law of Life rewards you openly!" I want to explain, because I hope We can roll it up now in a ball in the Violet Flame and consume it forever, and release all of your feelings from this thing that you have considered a problem about the age limit of the "I AM" Ascended Master Youth. You know, if you let that thing get going, personal feeling rides high; and when you get through, you still haven't solved your problem, have you? Aren't you still faced with this one and that one every so often saying, "Well, am I eligible?" or "Can I come in if I'm this age, or that age?" or something else?

Let Me tell you the Law. And this married and single problem—you must get out of yourselves and look back upon yourselves, and you will learn a lot. You can be married and as pure as the Heart of the Central Sun; and you can be unmarried and as filthy as the compound. Now the Law is the Law, and that's a matter for every individual to decide within himself or herself; and unless you do keep your innermost secret thoughts and feelings and pictures in your mind as pure as the Heart of the Central Sun, if you will do that, then you will find all things around you becoming that Purity and that Light and that Joyous Perfection that is the Authority of Freedom. And Precious Ones, that's the only Authority and Freedom in all the Universe! Your "Mighty I AM Presence" can't give you Perfection in your outer affairs or in your minds and bodies unless the Purity of Its own Heart's Flame, which is the Love from the Great Central Sun, floods into you and purifies all the energy of your emotional bodies and your mental bodies, and removes from your mind and the atmosphere about you the pictures that are not Purity and Perfection.

Mankind have gone on, Precious Ones, like an ostrich with its head in the sand, imagining they can go on and misuse this Great Energy of Life and not be found out; and all the time something comes along and bowls them over from behind, and they are in another turmoil, they are in another war.

Now please, don't be an ostrich. You're "I AM" Students! If you want the Truth, We will tell It to you! If you don't, you will have to go to the outer world and suffer it out, that's all; but he who won't listen to the Truth, he who will not conquer that outer self, is in for distress—I don't mind telling you. There are forces playing upon mankind's mental and feeling worlds in the next few months that, I tell you, are diabolical in the extreme; and unless you are filled with and armored by Our Eternal, Invincible Cosmic Christ Love, and that Victorious Purity which "I AM" to the Earth now, you won't have the Strength to stand against that condition of the outer world which is rampant everywhere.

If you take your Stand and turn your backs upon everything except Our Victory, you will find Our Strength in you to make you Victorious! If you are determined your "Mighty I AM Presence" shall have all, and It shall come into yourselves and reveal the Beauty and Perfection of Its Glory, and be Its Joyous, Victorious Accomplishment in everything in this World—if you want to be or release Its Mastery over things in this World, then My Dear Ones, We are there to assist you! We are there to protect you! We are there to supply you with every good thing. We are there to lift you above every turmoil; but I plead with you, do not use the tools of the sinister force and then expect the Protection of the Ascended Masters, because you will not have It. I'm not going to leave you in any misunderstanding about these

things that come under the Great Law and control of
the energy of the Universe.

If you use the slightest element of deceit, you
have placed yourself under the law of the sinister
force. There is no such thing as "a little white lie."
There never was, there never will be! Anything that
isn't Truth is untruth, and every untruth contains
within itself penalty. The Messenger told you the
other night: you get the reputation for standing un-
flinching on what you know to be right, and do not
yield an inch; and you will go forward from one
mighty Victory to another, and the sinister force will
fear you and, ultimately, dare not approach. All you
have to take is your unshakable Stand with the Perfection of your "Mighty I AM Presence," and know
that It is the Authority to command and to compel
everything that is of human feeling, human discord,
human plans, human ideas to be forced into the
Violet Consuming Flame by your Command; and it
shall be so.

You are not at the mercy of these forces of the
outer world, My Dear Ones! You have Legions of
Ascended Master Friends who guard you like diamonds, because every one of you is an Open Door
through which Our Light and Purity and Cosmic
Christ Love can flood into the atmosphere of Earth,
wherever you abide; and you might just as well get

the reputation now for being inflexibly and immovably firm in your decision.

If you are right and you know you are right, take your Stand; and as We have reminded you again and again, don't side-step an issue and don't hedge. When people ask you a direct question, give a direct answer; and if you don't, you are just caught in this outer world thing. The outer world has so long thought it could hide something; and people don't hide a thing, Dear Ones. That old human intellect, it is so hypnotized, self-hypnotized by its own imaginary power, which is but temporary energy because it has no eternally sustained supply of energy. It has imagined so long that it can hide something. It has gone on and on in its brazen conceit and gotten into deeper distress all the time.

People think they hide things from others. They may not tell them, and they may fawn upon somebody else; but underneath, if it's in the feeling world—you are standing in each other's atmosphere, and your feeling world extends for at least a radius of fifty feet around the physical body in every direction; so, anybody that stands in your feeling world feels your feeling. Therefore, there is no such thing as fooling the "Presence" or fooling the Law or fooling Us. The intellect has preferred to fool itself, but it really hasn't fooled the people around the individual.

People become sensitive to these things; and don't you know discord—when you step into somebody's atmosphere who's angry? They may not say a word, but don't you know it? Don't you feel it when you come near? Well, so does everybody else feel you.

If somebody has got a wrong motive, sooner or later it reveals itself. And if you will stand with that Call for the All-Seeing Eye of God, the All-Knowing Mind of God, the Almighty Light of God to command and know that you are, at all times, illumined by the Mighty Ascended Masters' Cosmic Pure Mind of God, and there is nothing hidden that is not revealed to you that you need to know to hold Invincible Protection for what is constructive, to fulfill the Divine Plan the Ascended Masters' Way and expand It, and to give the Assistance to all who want to try to serve the Light.

Now, if you will do this and go on as if the sinister force didn't exist, except to shut it out every time there is a temporary appearance, you will go forward, Precious Ones. You can cut your way in the midst of a veritable jungle by this Conscious Command to Life, because it isn't your outer self that is doing all this. You let the "Presence" come in, or the Higher Mental Body blaze Its Flame and Its Light Rays into the outer self; and those Light Rays go before you to clear the conditions that otherwise would be your human struggle. And if you will armor yourselves with Our Eternal, Invincible Purity and Our Authority of Freedom to the Earth, Our Authority of the Cosmic Christ, which means the "Mighty I AM Presence" in the Great Central Sun, that Authority manifests as a Flame always.

You shall be armored in That! Your "I AM" Ascended Master Youth Headquarters can be filled with It. Your own individual business activities can be so charged with It, day after day. You can demand the increase of It a thousandfold every hour, or every day; and if you stand and charge and give your Life into That, qualified that way, that's the way Life will come back to you. And all it takes is the removal of your attention, the disconnection of your attention from the discordant conditions or the limitations of the outer world long enough to give the Command; and then you go about your business, and you will find that Wave of Light has gone before you and will do what you, on the physical side, cannot do.

We are determined, Precious Ones, to make you the Victory for which We call. We are not going to let down one second on the "I AM" Ascended Master Youth, because We will guard you, provided you are through experimenting with misery in the outer world. If you don't believe Us, if you don't believe We are Real, if you don't want to obey this

Law, well, that's quite all right with Us. Go to the outer world. Suffer it out as long as you please; that's your privilege, with which We have no desire to interfere—except when you get miserable enough, I think you will remember Us. You usually do.

We have found that all through the centuries; and the outer world hasn't done anything except to experiment with misery ever since the end of the second Golden Age. Every time a Great Being of Light has come and given a Transcendent Gift, most of the time He or She has been persecuted or crucified, or next door to it, during the lifetime; and then later on things have been reversed.

But you will find the outer world will not offer you one thing but misery, distress, and limitation if you don't stand and clothe yourselves in the Cosmic Christ Love from the Great Central Sun, and then blaze that Light into the world around you, so that you build your world out here according to the Perfection of the Law! Then, if you fill your world with the Mighty Christ Love of your "I AM Presence" and from Our Octave, well then, your Electronic Circle—which is your world, your Sphere of Life—becomes filled with Our Perfection and Our Power to help you accomplish anything you require to live in this World, and still go forth to your Victory and your Freedom. But if a thing is going to live in your world, Precious Ones, it either lives by your Life or it doesn't live.

Just make up your mind, whatever you want to do or manifest in the outer life has to live by your Life or it is not in your world; and you should think deeply upon that to which you want to give your Life. Everything in your Electronic Circle, every-thing in your world of affairs, either lives because you put your energy into it, which is your Life—and your Life is the Love from your "Presence," and your "Presence" is the Love and the Flame from the Great Central Sun. Therefore, whatever you want to do in the outer, you may do because Love is All-Powerful; but you have to give it your attention and pour that energy into it, qualified with Cosmic Christ Love and the Ascended Masters' Perfection if it is to be sus-tained or expanded, because unless it is Perfection, it is not worthy to exist in the Universe, and We cannot give Our Energy to something that is not construc-tive. That's self-evident!

We cannot use discordant energy. We cannot use tired energy. So may I plead with you, and when you give your Decrees, give them with happiness and joy, and a fierce determination to have that Perfec-tion; or get your rest first, and then give them. But don't drag around, one foot after the other, and then expect your Decrees fulfilled, and wonder why Perfection doesn't manifest.

Now I am going to say something, because We are going to stress this several times. It's quite necessary that new people coming into the Activity understand this; and those who have been in the Activity, if it has been a habit, well, correct it, that's all—and that is to please watch the tone of your voice. Please watch the quality that you put into your voice; and as you live and breathe and want anything decent, for Heaven's sake, stop a whine in the voice! There is nothing so irritating, there is nothing such a wide-open negative invitation to the whole sinister force, as a whine in the voice.

It's irritating to the nerves. It is a let-down in the energy. It's wholly negative; and it has no business to be in the Universe, that's all! Now, the tones of the voice that heal, the tones of the voice that are positive, that do the things that are worthwhile doing, are in the middle register; and those of you who sing, We will experiment with you someday, and show you by actual experience inside of your own selves, the difference in the vibratory action of those middle tones in your voice and the deeper tones, and the effect of the high shrill tones.

We can show you this on the tape recorders. We can show them to you on your bells, or anything else. And if the Student Body will remember this, your words will carry a lot more power. You will speak with a greater conviction, and you will be far more convincing to people of the outer world in anything you want to accomplish if you will remember this. So far as your singing voices are concerned, they will improve tremendously if you keep a good, positive, happy register or quality going into the middle register of your voices.

You can heal, sometimes, by one spoken word. The moment people become irritated or angry, the voice rises. When it rises, it becomes shrill. Anger manifests always in the high register, and you never heard anybody give a command that others obeyed that they didn't speak in the lower tones of the voice.

Now, these are just mechanical things that will help you to keep shut out the conditions that are irritating in the outer world; and as "I AM" Ascended Master Youth, if you will make up your minds now what you actually want to do at your Headquarters, and you will call to Us—remember, the Seven Mighty Elohim are the Builders of the System. We still know how to build—you'd be surprised! And We don't build anything that isn't beautiful. We don't build anything that couldn't be sustained forever, and what We build is Our Gift to you.

If you want to build as We do, and if you want Our Love with which to build, if you want Our Protection to that which you build through Love, and you want it to render its service to Life to help beautify the Planet—the sky is the limit! There is nobody in the physical octave that can offer you That! They might think they could give you the sky, but they can't.

As you make up your minds as to what you want to do, set your pattern, and get the Picture clear—then love that Picture with all your Heart, with all your mind, with all your feeling, with all the energy of your being! Command in the Name and Authority of your "Mighty I AM Presence"! Demand It come into outer manifestation by the Authority and Power of the Mightiest Cosmic Christ Love of all Creation. Then ask Us, as the Seven Mighty Builders, to stand the Guard, to see that what you build is built perfectly, that it renders a tremendous service, it never can produce anything but happiness for all concerned; and it's worthy of everything you will ever have, all the rest of Eternity, to give it, to expand it, to protect it, and to pour forth through it that which blesses your fellowman.

And then—now this might seem that you are going to be busy for a long while ahead; but you might just as well know that it is part of your business now to remember that every city that is to be sustained into the future, and all the new ones that are to come forth, you will have to have some hand in the building. You might have many Cities of Light to be built; and if you practice and do this present service well, who are you to say what We will give you? Who are you to say what We will draw forth for your use that does not yet exist in the physical octave?

Love is not limited! Life is not limited! Energy is not limited! Consciousness is not limited, at least Ours isn't; and We are trying to give you Ours in the place of yours.

Now, it's more than an even trade, but if you will give Us yours, We'll give you Ours. But We aren't going to use yours! We're going to put it in the Violet Flame. So that's My Way of purifying your mental body; and if you will give Us your feelings of disturbance and distress and limitation, We'll give you Our Feelings of the Love of the Cosmic Christ! Now, that's another trade! This is a business proposition today. We are going into business together, aren't we? We are the Builders, and you are the builders. We might be the Architects, but you will have to handle the bricks; but don't throw them at each other! We want you to go forward like happy children and build with freedom, but with a confidence that Love alone can bestow, and you will know what Mastery is. You might just as well know it now, as ten years from now, or fifty years.

You don't have to wait for your Ascension in order to observe what Mastery is; and you will have a lot more joy and a great deal more Mastery over this World by contemplating It now, than you will just before your Ascension. That might be the Completion of It; but you can enjoy many, many, many of Its wonderful Powers in your outer physical use, years before your Ascension is attained. We alone can give you the Feeling of that Mastery which is Ours!

If you are a musician, you can give your student your feeling of a musical composition; and the student, getting quiet, can absorb your feeling and play like you. And We can give you Our Feeling of the Builders of Creation. We can give you Our Feeling of Mastery, and this is the most wonderful Blessing of all: We can give you Our Feeling of Love to someone you don't like! Did you ever think of that? Sometimes, when it seems difficult to pour Cosmic Christ Love to someone that you think isn't worthy of it or is doing something aggravating, if you call to Us, We can flash the Flame of Our Love to that Life Stream—at least to the "Presence" and Higher Mental Body, and to all that's constructive in it. We can flash Our Flame of Love to that individual, and do things on the moment that you could not quite do because perhaps your feelings might not be governed for the moment; but We can help you to govern them.

Now then, let Us build first the Perfection within yourselves, by your Calls for that Cosmic Christ Love from the Great Central Sun that is Master Authority everywhere, that "Mighty I AM Presence" whose Love and Life in the Great Central Sun is Master throughout all the Universe. Call It into yourselves until It qualifies your energy; and then call Our Love, Our Love and Our Mastery, Our Invincible Purity, and Our Authority into and through and around yourselves, and go forward and build the Fulfillment of the Divine Plan. Contemplate everything that you build with its effect, or its capacity to bring happiness to others; and you are bound to become happy yourself.

If you accept Our Partnership and if you like Our Way of Life, We can show you Designs that have never yet been on this Earth, but that are Beautiful beyond words to describe, and things that are going to come into outer action in the permanent Golden Age. You can be the recipients of those Gifts! You can carry the Gifts of that Beauty into outer manifestation and have joy every step of the way.

Now, if you want to qualify this year with the Victory of Our Ascended Master Joy, Our Great Cosmic Christ Joy of Eternal Love, Invincible Purity, the Mighty Boundless Supply of every good thing, and you *demand the Authority of Eternal, Invincible Freedom of the "Mighty I AM Presence" to take you forward and build as the Ascended Ones do,* We will be with you. The building will go forward. You will have what you require, and the outer world can stand and take its surprise. We are with you! The outer world is against you. And if you don't believe it, experiment with both; and when you are through with the outer, come to Us. But you don't need to look there anymore if you should choose to come to Us first. We can take you forward to what the outer world can never give.

So, as We move forward, feel with all the Power of your beings Our Reality, *feel* the Power of Our Love to give you every good thing; and be aware of Us. Associate with Our Thoughts and Feelings. *Demand to be charged with Our Power of Victorious Accomplishment, and demand that the Authority of Our Cosmic Freedom of Eternal, Invincible Cosmic Christ Love and Purity moves your Victory before you;* and everywhere you go, success is at hand, and the outer world cannot interfere with Us nor That which We give. We want you to be free from, independent of, and wholly untouched by the limitations of the outer world. Love alone can give That, and Our Sacred Fire is the Fullness of Its Authority and Its Victorious Presence.

Thank you. And as I enfold you in Its Blazing Flame, I demand you become aware of It, and know that It abides with you to give you Joy and Perfection and Freedom without limit, into the Fullness of your Ascension.

Thank you.

(Record CD 1369)

Excerpts on the Elohim of Purity

Beloved Saint Germain

The more Purity you want, the more you will have to contemplate Purity. Without your attention upon It and your conscious Call for It, only a small portion of It flows into your world. There is a certain natural flow of It from your "Presence," but you can intensify that beyond all measure by commanding your attention to go to the Elohim, that Glorious, Magnificent Presence of Eternal Invincible Purity, a Being whose Garments are of White Fire, whose Radiance is like White Lightning, and whose Love responds perhaps more quickly than any other one of the Great Cosmic Beings. Do you feel It? Will you accept It? . . .

He is the Light of Eternal Invincible Purity! He is the Great Cosmic Powerhouse or Pressure of Purity which is drawn from the Great Central Sun! . . .

Outside of the Knowledge of the "I AM Presence" and the use of the Violet Flame, through which My Freedom comes, mankind need this Mighty Elohim of Eternal Invincible Purity to pour forth His Pressure of the Cosmic Power which He wields, more than anything on this Earth today. They need It

more than they need food! They need It more than
they need air! . . .

O Great Elohim of Eternal Invincible Purity,
purify the structure of these bodies! Purify the mental and feeling world! Purify the atmosphere wherever they move. Make them Thy Living Self in Action, and release Thy Cosmic Pressure of Eternal
Invincible Purity throughout America. Purify everything within Her borders and take Thy Dominion!
Thou Great Builder of Creation, Thou art the Cor-
nerstone of the Universe!

("Voice of the I AM," January 1944)

CHAPTER X
Beloved Elohim of Purity

Shasta Springs, California
September 19, 1968

Beloved Ones of Our Hearts, I trust I may bring you Assistance tonight in a way that will be very practical, and I trust will make your pathway easier and your control of outer world conditions more Victorious; and it is this.

If you will *demand and command, before you go to sleep at night and when you first awaken in the morning, simply with every atom of your being, demand that your "Beloved I AM Presence" and the Ascended Host hold the Ascended Masters' Control of your attention, and keep it away from anything that would draw destruction into your world.*

I have a very important reason for asking for this, because it will give Us a certain use of the Sacred Fire from Our own Hearts' Flame through your own brain structure; and in doing that, it will clear out many, many concepts that you have accepted, past and present. Sometimes you don't even know that you accept the feeling of conditions that are wrong in the outer world. This is to protect your emotional bodies from being stirred up, or stirred into action on destructive conditions, because the attention has gone to those conditions; and while your attention is upon them, it is pouring the destructively qualified feeling in those conditions into your own Life Stream, of your own emotional body.

Therefore, if you will *ask your "Mighty I AM Presence" first, always, and then the Ascended Masters' Diamond-Shining Control of your attention that keeps it off of mistakes and problems and that which is wrong,* you will feel a very great relief in the pressure in your own feeling world. This will bring a Peace within you that will make you feel your own Power and Victory over conditions that have been of distress, past or present.

There must be some concerted action in each of you, by your own conscious Call, to cut yourselves free from every destructive etheric record—whether it be of yourselves or someone else, matters not. And Our Sacred Fire Purity, Our Fiery Christ Blue-Lightning Purity is, I assure you, the complete Master Control of all the energy in your feeling word if you will so command it. But your attention is the thing, because it wanders here, there, everywhere; and if you allow it to rest upon destructive conditions that other people have generated, and maybe have touched your Life Streams—you can just as well seal yourselves within the Ascended Masters' Control of your attention as to let it run wild, and let the destructive forces drive into you more and more of their destruction, until you of your own Free Will close the door of Eternity.

Now the reason I say this is because, in the Ascended Masters' Octave, We have to keep Our Attention off the mistakes and problems of the past, or they would become immortal in Our World; and that cannot be! And if you will, every time you look at the Sun, feel your own "Mighty I AM Presence'" Heart Flame reach up and thank all the Life and the Light of the Physical Sun for Its Love to the Earth; and ask your "Beloved I AM Presence" to hold Control of your attention and the feeling of the outer self, by the Diamond-Shining Love of the "Mighty I AM Presence," the Ascended Host, the Physical Sun, the Great Central Sun—anything that reveals to you what Light manifests in the magnificent Cosmic Activities of the Infinite Universe.

Every time you think of Light in the physical world, remember two things—and I am not speaking of a lurid red glow, because that is the destructive force's accumulation of more destruction—I am speaking of clear, dazzling White Light, and also the Light, the colors, in the spectrum. When you see a rainbow or the beautiful, clean, clear colors in the Powers of Nature and Forces of the Elements, remind your intellect that they are some manifestation of Love; and that Love is Indestructible, Eternal Purity, because mankind can never change the Cosmic Law that creates those manifestations by Love alone. And that Love is the Heart Flame of the Great Central Sun. As It pours Its Presence throughout all the Systems of Worlds that come under Its Direction, It gives of Itself—Its Eternal Purity, Perfection, and Love.

That Sacred Fire Presence is everywhere pouring Its Love and Perfection to Life. It is pouring Its Infinite Music in the atmosphere of your World—the upper atmosphere—and It is pouring the Power without limit of the Sacred Fire Love from the Great Central Sun; and you cannot produce any manifestation without the use of Power. But the majority of mankind's concepts of Power are not that that Power is either luminosity or is the Love of the Purity from the Great Central Sun.

If you will qualify everything that you contact in outer physical conditions as mistakes or problems or things that seem to be wrong—if you will simply keep calling into them the "Mighty I AM Presence" and the Ascended Masters' Sacred Fire Purity of such Cosmic Power that it forces the Purification that dissolves and consumes the mistake, or the problem, or the destructive etheric record, or the focus of energy and substance that is manifesting as destruction.

Now, this has a very powerful effect in the atmosphere in which you live, whether it be in your own room or your home or your business or outer world activities. If you will continually call to your "Mighty I AM Presence," periodically during the day—you don't need to sit in contemplation upon It all the time—call for It before you go to sleep at night; acknowledge It and demand It when you awaken in the morning. Then in the midst of outer world conditions, remember It, so It can come forth as a Flash of Flame into a mistake or a problem, or conditions of the outer world, and consume the impurity; and if It consumes the impurity, It will consume the thing that causes the limitation or the distress by the problem. But destructive etheric records must be consumed by the Sacred Fire if Purity is to take their place and produce Manifestation that is the Fulfillment of the Divine Plan, or that is constructive for mankind's use anywhere in the physical world.

Now this has tremendous blessing and effect upon your health! People do not fill themselves with the Ascended Masters' Sacred Fire Purifying Love or Indestructible Purity! Every time something is of discord in the outer self, the attention and the habit, past and present, of mankind's *acceptance* of limitation and distress is the first reaction to the awareness of that distress by your intellect or by your feeling. So, no

matter what is wrong, someday, sometime, somewhere, it must be consumed by the Sacred Fire's Indestructible Purifying Love. Your Violet Consuming
Flame is That! Your Unfed Flame is Love, Wisdom,
and Power held forever within the Indestructible Purity of the Great Central Sun.

The Sevenfold Flames of the Seven Mighty
Elohim are all the Purifying Love from the Great
Central Sun! No matter what Quality you want, no
matter what Power you want to use in the physical
world, form the habit of recognizing, first, the Sacred
Fire's Love of Indestructible Purity. And if you will
charge This into anything and everything you contact, there will come such Freedom to you, such
Blessings, and such relief from limitations as I cannot
put into words until you begin to use It.

Form the habit when there seems to be a sudden battle between individuals—whether it be controversy or just general opposition—whenever you are
aware of it, *call instantly to your "Mighty I AM Presence"
and the Ascended Host to flash there the Diamond-Shining
Indestructible Purity that controls it!* And My Dear Ones,
you can be such a Blessing to Life. You can have
such Power to use in the unascended state to correct
conditions down here, that you can only understand
as you use It. And then you become It; and wherever you go, We could pour forth through you more

and more of that Sacred Fire's Indestructible Purity to consume conditions when you pass by, and you not even know that that consuming takes place. We can flash That in and around you into conditions in the atmosphere that are invisible to you, and yet they are destructive.

We are making this Call and giving you this Explanation for more than just your own personal convenience and Mastery and Victory of the Ascension. This World—no matter what the problem is that has to be solved, *every problem in this World can only be solved by placing within it enough Sacred Fire Indestructible Purity,* to allow that which is constructive to unite and become the Manifestation of the Perfection that fulfills the Divine Plan, so that as soon as you set the habit of calling night and morning and in the middle of the day—it only takes an instant—but when you call into outer physical conditions the Ascended Masters' Sacred Fire Love's Indestructible Purity, you will consume the destructive conditions that have been generated by hate. You will consume the destructive etheric records; and in that consuming there will continually build within and around you the Indestructible Purity of Cosmic Light-Substance from the Ascended Masters' Octave that is Crystal Clear. It's just like sunshine on diamonds; and It is so hard no destructive thing can ever come through it.

If you will do this—and remember, whenever you think of your Mighty Magic Electronic Tube of Cosmic Light-Substance, and you qualify That as the Ascended Masters' Sacred Fire Love's Indestructible Purity, the Diamond-Shining Substance from the Ascended Masters' Octave that is so blazing with Its Indestructible Purity that no one can see who abides within—that is, no destructive activity. Therefore, It becomes for you not only greater and greater Protection, but It is continually in action, repelling and consuming destructive forces around you. And you will find, one day, That becomes a Sun Presence, or an Oval of Dazzling Light-Substance around you, in which you can move anywhere you please. It lights your way. It is a Reservoir of Indestructible Power—Power that nothing human can oppose.

If I can get you to set this habit, I will armor you from tonight with a Power that you will never understand until you use It and you become It. And then you will begin to realize and feel, really, what Freedom is; and you never will feel completely free until this Blazing Sacred Fire's Indestructible Purity becomes an Eternal Part of your Life Stream, expands Its Flame without limit, stands around you Its Cosmic Light-Substance, and continues to repel and consume the hordes of evil wherever you might pass by.

It is Power, My Dear Ones, without limit. And when you just keep calling forth whatever Indestructible Purity of the Sacred Fire consumes every destructive etheric record, the Cosmic Law not only consumes it within you first, but It will consume the destructive etheric records in the structure of the Earth that have been concentrated here from centuries past of mankind's frightful conditions generated by war.

When you think of the warring conditions of the World, *call the "Beloved Mighty I AM Presence" of every Life Stream in existence in this World, embodied now, as well as the Ascended Host, to blaze into those warring conditions whatever Great Central Sun's Sacred Fire Love's Indestructible Purity makes war impossible of existence, impossible of manifestation, impossible of being continued by anybody or anything in any government in the World!* And this is vitally necessary for your Protection as a Nation. *(applause)* Thank you so much. Won't you be seated, please; and just remain so.

Now, in the conferences of the various nations of the World, in outer world activities, when you know something is going on that's wrong, don't hesitate to call forth the mightiest Sacred Fire Indestructible Purity in the Great Central Sun, the Physical Sun, and from the Ascended Masters' Octave, to concentrate into those conditions whatever indestructible

Purity compels the prevention of all wrong. This must come forth and be established as an Eternal Part of the Earth, because one day the Sacred Fire must be established and pass through every bit of substance of which the planet Earth is composed. And that Substance must be charged with Sacred Fire Indestructible Purity, in order to release Its Blessings through the Powers of Nature and Forces of the Elements, to sustain mankind here in the future, and to fulfill the Great Divine Plan of illumining the Earth.

Now, if you set this habit and begin to gain this momentum, many times perhaps when you least expect it, there will come a certain Illumination around you, in the atmosphere about you sometimes, that will surprise you and make you feel that the atmosphere about you is not as dark as ordinarily it has seemed. We want This about you for many reasons. It's a very powerful Healing Activity within and around you; and if you want your bodies Self-Luminous, you must command it. You must say so. You must love that Sacred Fire's Indestructible Purity into yourselves, and you will find It will love you into Perfection and there is no such thing as failure.

When you call forth from the Great Central Sun as well as your "Mighty I AM Presence" and the Ascended Host, the Great Central Sun's Heart Flame's Love of Indestructible Purity, and demand It fill everything in your being and world with Its Almighty Perfection forever, and then is established around you and wherever you go, It keeps consuming, consuming, consuming the hordes of evil; and then you become the Illumining Presence of the "Mighty I AM"–Its Almighty Outpouring of anything and everything It wishes to accomplish through you, wherever It moves you in outer physical conditions.

Now in the business world, there is so much filth in many offices and outer world activities that just holds people bound to slavery and disaster and destruction and lack and limitation. Whenever these things come to your attention, make this Call. And if you want to call It forth as the Great Central Sun's Heart Flame of Fiery Christ Blue-Lightning Indestructible Purity into those conditions, and increase It until that which is wrong has been consumed, you will find many conditions improving in outer world business channels that certainly need to be purified for everybody's Blessing.

You cannot do anything but have greater and greater Blessing by calling This forth, both around yourselves and into outer physical conditions, wherever you pass, even the structure of the Earth. Call forth the Great Central Sun's Heart Flame's Love of such Indestructible Purity that It is planted, so to speak, into the structure of Earth to consume every-thing that is of discord; and you can be a Blessing to Life everywhere you move. But to make you feel the greater Protection of your own Mighty Magic Elec-tronic Tube of Cosmic Light-Substance, keep ac-knowledging It as the Diamond-Shining Substance from the Ascended Masters' Octave, because you don't provide that Substance from the physical world. That comes from your "Beloved I AM Presence" or the Ascended Masters. Call Its Diamond-Shining Substance of Indestructible Purity that will not let anything human come through; and I tell you, Pre-cious Ones, you can have Power unlimited if you will remember to do this.

Now if you will accept this, it will make the ac-complishment very much quicker and, I am sure, more comfortable for you; and that is to *charge your own memories with the Ascended Masters' Diamond-Shining Memory of Indestructible, Protecting Perfection.* And if you will use It, you won't follow the habit of the outer world's loss of memory. You will not become senile. You will not become incapacitated. You will not be-come part of the outer world's barnacles of incapacity because the outer self has simply accepted, accepted, accepted limitation and distress. Don't let that habit remain within you, of every time you can't think, say-ing, "Well, I can't remember." Well, you'd better remember the Source from whence you came, or you'll never be Free! And you can *charge yourselves with such Ascended Master Diamond-Shining Memory of Indestructible Purity, that no destructive thing can be imposed upon your consciousness by any destructive activity for any reason whatsoever.* This will clear every faculty of the mind.

You can do the same thing in your feeling. *Command your feeling to be filled with the Diamond-Shining, Indestructible Purity of the Love from the Great Central Sun that manifests Perfection throughout infinite space!* You can have This! It is in existence. All It asks is your Call from the physical octave, because We may not intrude on your Free Will. If you will call of your own Free Will for Indestructible Purity in, through, and around all you contact, We can establish It in the Mightiest Power that you could ever require, and greater than mankind has ever known, past or present. It's yours for use, free as the air you breathe! *(applause)* Thank you so much, Precious Ones.

As long as limitation remains, and discord and impurity in the outer world, this Call needs to go forth constantly as the Solution of every problem, as the Correction of all mistakes, and as the Removal from the Nation of the filth that seeks to destroy and desecrate it.

And those conditions can only be removed by the Sacred Fire's Indestructible Purity, and your Violet Consuming Flame is that. But the Sevenfold Flame of the Seven Mighty Elohim can govern the qualities in the activities and the powers of your intellect, including your memory. It can govern all the energy in your feeling world and cut you free from the torture that human creation has imposed upon you as destructive habits, past or present, or the acceptance of outer world limitation.

So, when you don't want to accept any limitation of the outer world, fill yourselves with your "Beloved I AM Presence" and the Ascended Host's Great Central Sun's Sacred Fire Love's Indestructible Purity, with the Conscious Command that It repels and consumes everything that is not that Love's Indestructible Purity; and wherever you go, you will live, move, and have your beings in all the Perfection God's Heart can give; and that is Sacred Fire Love without limit for Eternity.

Please don't waste your time or keep your attention on destructive conditions mankind has generated, past or present. But instead when they come to your attention, flash the Fiery Christ Blue-Lightning Indestructible Purity, and ask your "Mighty I AM Presence" to establish It, or an Ascended Being; and you will find you can clear the atmosphere wherever you go.

Now This has a very Powerful Effect, is the reason I am bringing It to your attention tonight for the consuming of hate in the atmosphere about you—or hate that has gotten into the emotional body from discord past or present—because hate must be consumed, and it can only be consumed by Sacred Fire Purity.

No matter where it is or who generates it or how long it has been in existence, or its destructive etheric records, there is only one thing that will take it out of the Universe, and that's Indestructible Purity. And as the Sacred Fire Love of that Indestructible Purity passes through, It can consume in a Flash hate that mankind has generated, perhaps for centuries! This is necessary to hold certain balance in the structure of the Earth. It is necessary to shut off war. It is necessary to prevent epidemics and disease, and it is necessary to produce Harmony and Success in outer world business channels that are constructive. And there isn't any human being on the Earth who will make that Call who won't be answered, because the greater Life in the Universe and the greatest Life in the Great Central Sun that has been poured to this System of Worlds throughout the ages has said from the very beginning, "Call unto Me, and I will answer thee!"

We can't say "No" if unascended beings will make the Call. And people don't need to stay in their chains if they will ask for Sacred Fire Love's Indestructible Purity to dissolve and consume everything that has caused distress to Life.

So if you will stand with Us, We will try and help to keep you reminded as often as possible—if you will use This in outer world conditions that come to your attention in the physical world that We want to remove from your Nation before they become any greater, or the destruction is allowed to destroy any more of the Blessings God has given you here.

This Nation must be purified! Mankind has no remedy for the discord and the destruction that has been generated. Mankind cannot stop destruction by more destruction, and just talking about it doesn't consume it. But I'll guarantee you, that when you call to your "Mighty I AM Presence" and the Ascended Host and the Great Beings in the Great Central Sun for the Sacred Fire Love's Indestructible Purity, We *can* call It forth into all creation; and It *will be* the Master Control of everything in the physical world. And It's the *only* Freedom there is!

That's the reason Beloved Saint Germain gave you the use of the Violet Consuming Flame, because

It is part of the Great Central Sun's Indestructible Purity. Mankind's impurity cannot come into the Violet Consuming Flame.

So from tonight, I want you to feel the Power, if you will, of All that Our Love can give, and Our Love can give more than you can comprehend in the intellect. This which I offer in the Call for Indestructible Purity to come into the feeling of mankind— where the destructive forces accumulate the most and do their greatest damage—when you call This into outer action to consume all destructive forces, there will come to your assistance Unconquerable, Limitless Legions of the Diamond-Shining Angels of such Fiery Christ Blue-Lightning Purity, mankind would stand speechless were they to see Them in Action. And I want Them to come into the lower atmosphere of Earth as soon as possible. *(applause)* Thank you so much.

You must have more Power in the physical octave than mankind can manage. You must have more Power in this Nation of Our Indestructible Purity of the Sacred Fire than there is energy in the destructive forces mankind has generated and imposed upon this Nation. You must have more of the Great Central Sun's Sacred Fire Love's Indestructible Purity than all the energy communism has qualified down here with destruction. There must come more from

Above if this is to be consumed and mankind set Free. And I assure you, the Divine Law is such that It *must* come, and as soon as possible!

From tonight I hope We may have your cooperation, because I am not going to say We're going to use you—We're not. We're going to cooperate with you; and when you want This for yourselves, We will enfold you in more from a Cosmic Angle that, wherever you pass by, can consume anything and everything of human creation when you call It into existence. And We are ready to give It without limit to purify your Nation, to save your Nation, and to prevent what the hordes of evil intend to desecrate throughout the World.

So, don't talk about destructive things, but call forth the Great Central Sun's Indestructible Purity that consumes them. Be the Master Presence that controls manifestation and issues the Great Command for evil to cease to be, by Fiery Christ Blue-Lightning Purity for all Eternity; and you can't fail!

There are limitless Legions of the Diamond-Shining Angels that can come into the lower physical atmosphere of Earth, and nobody can tell Me what moment They might become Visible to all! *(applause)* Thank you so much.

Since Indestructible Purity is My Service to Life, and the Indestructible Victory of that Indestructible

Purity is Power Unlimited, I am willing to give It to anybody and everybody who will call It forth to purify the Nation, and help free the Earth and hold it at peace. Then you, of yourselves, must automatically become Free.

If you will use It for the Nation and the World, We automatically can lift you out of the clutches of any condition that has been imposed upon you by human creation, no matter what the cause.

So from tonight, if you will keep acknowledging Our Diamond-Shining Indestructible Purity to come and come and come, and possess every condition in the physical word that doesn't yield Perfection and Purity for Eternity, you will find Us very Tangible; and you will find the Help We give, Invincible for Eternity.

Tonight We clothe you again in Our Diamond-Shining Miracle Mantle of such Indestructible Sacred Fire Purity from the Great Central Sun, that It will keep you Invincible and lift you out of the discord and out of the connection with discordant conditions, until you make this Call and your own momentum clothes you in a Powerhouse that you can use wherever you abide the rest of Eternity. And We can clothe you in whatever helps your Nation and the World as powerfully as possible at this time. We thank you if you will, of your own Free Will, call

This into all outer physical conditions. We will make it plain to the world where the Victory of Light is, who directs It, and who has Its Power to use to control physical conditions, that sets the rest of Life Free; and you will not find Us wanting!

All We ask is that, of your own Free Will, you want Indestructible Purity of Our Sacred Fire Love. Call It into action in and around yourselves; charge everything with Its Diamond-Shining Victory; and let Us have the opening to free the Nation and the World, as quickly as possible, from the desecrating forces that are trying everywhere to destroy and desecrate all the Blessings the "Mighty I AM Presence" and the Ascended Host have placed in this World.

So, from tonight We want to clothe you in Our Armor of the Sacred Fire's Indestructible Purity from the Great Central Sun, to illumine your way, protect you without limit, and help you to purify the Earth wherever you abide. And if you will cooperate with Us, you will find We can and will fulfill every Call, until this World is a Diamond-Shining Presence of Invincible Purity for Eternity, and the Sacred Fire Love has drawn to Itself Its own.

We clothe you in Its Heart Flame; and may Its Almighty, Victorious Presence illumine your way and make you the Diamond-Shining Freedom from all that is wrong, everywhere you abide the rest of Eternity. Thank you with all My Heart.

(Record CD 1472)

CHAPTER XI
Beloved Elohim Hercules

Philadelphia, Pennsylvania
November 10, 1952

Beloved Ones in the Heart of Freedom, may I offer you tonight an Explanation of those Activities of Divine Love that are your release from everything in this World that causes you distress or limitation. And since you live in the City of Brotherly Love, let us understand what that Love is. You see, you must become an exponent of Its Majesty and Its Power; and since you are in the actual Focus of Its Flame, you shouldn't be able to express anything else.

Now, I am supposed to be a Being of Great Strength and Power; and I trust I am! But what Strength and Power is it, do you think, that gives Me the Cosmic Opportunity to create Cosmic Conditions that bless Life through a whole System of Worlds? Because of the Power of that Love through which I have attained.

Now, when you understand that your Freedom from the limitations of this outer world comes only by your attention going to your "Blessed I AM

Presence" in love, your attention carrying your love there, your attention coming to Our Octave—then from Our Octave must come the Power of Love to draw you out of connection with that which has been of discord through the centuries.

Now in understanding the Power of the Great Central Sun Magnet, I wish you to remember this: the Power of that Magnet is the drawing activity of the Love from the Great Central Sun. So when your love goes to that Great Central Sun Magnet, the very flow of the energy of your Life, qualified with love to that Great Central Sun and to Its Great Magnet—that, in itself, is a Raising Power and Raising Activity to the atomic structure of the physical body. And now let Me show you how magnificent is that Power when you call It forth into your affairs.

You know the action of a magnet is to draw to itself, isn't it? Then, when you send your love to that Great Central Sun Magnet, your own love draws you there through your attention. The Love in that Central Sun Magnet draws you to Itself. Therefore, when you call Its Action, Its Authority, and Its Power into physical conditions, Its natural action is to draw that substance and that energy into the Flame of Its own Love in order to make that substance and energy Eternal Love.

So, My Dear Ones, your obligation to Life for
your own Freedom is, first of all, your love to your
"Presence" and to the Ascended Host, to the Great
Central Sun and the Physical Sun. But in your service to mankind, My Dear Ones, your whole duty is to
teach mankind to love that "Mighty I AM Presence"
and the Divine Beings who are the Focus of Its
Power, and are the Magnetic Action of Its Presence to
draw them out of the conditions they have created
which were not love. So, you will only have one
thing to teach mankind: first of all, the existence of
this "Blessed Mighty I AM Presence," which is *One*
with all the Ascended Masters. *To teach mankind to love
that "Presence" and the Ascended Host is the greatest understanding you could bring to Life!*

Every activity of that "Presence" is an Activity
of Love! Its Gift of the Violet Consuming Flame is
the Purifying Power of Its Love. The Gift of Its
Mighty Word "I AM", as the Great Creative Word
of the Universe, is the Gift of Its Power of Love to
create manifestation. The Gift of Its Intelligence is
the All-Knowing Flame of Love from the Great Central Sun.

So your service to Life, My Dear Ones, both for
your own Freedom and that of your fellowman, is to
teach everybody and everything you contact to love
the "Mighty I AM Presence" and the Ascended Host,

because that Love is the Power that draws everybody or everything that places its attention There, up and out of the vibratory action of this World and into the Love of Its Eternal Perfection.

So, in carrying this Light of the Ascended Masters' Instruction of the "Mighty I AM Presence," My Dear Ones, the Radiation which comes through the actual Words of the Ascended Host is a Flame as well as a Substance; and It is also the Radiation of the Light Rays from the Flame. And those Light Rays must penetrate the substance of the brain structure and the energy of the feeling world, which flows into the individual through the Heart and through the solar plexus, the stomach.

Now, you all know that the energy at the stomach is the first place that feels fear, irritation, distress, anger, depression, or anything that is a discordant feeling. The first place it strikes is the stomach; and this is because the great accumulation of energy there, through the food that is placed in it every day, makes it the target or point of contact for the destructive forces.

Now, if you will practice sending your love to the "Presence," and send your love to the Great Central Sun Magnet, and ask It to draw you away from everything that is not Its Eternal Victory of that Love—I tell you frankly, Precious Ones, when you

can feel the necessity of teaching all mankind to love
the Life that is greater than themselves, if they would
only pour the love There, they would rise out of their
limitations. They have loved their human desires a
long while; and they have held their attention on
those human desires, and their discord has bound
them to the substance of this World. They have created that discord here in this octave; and through
that, they bind themselves and anchor themselves
and hold themselves here in their limitations because
they will not give the love There that is the magnetic
pull to draw them out of their limitation.

So I tell you, Precious Ones, the Supreme Service to Life is to teach Life that has been bound by
mankind's human creation into the substance that is
qualified with discord. You must teach mankind to
love the Life from whence they come, the greater Life
that controls the Universe; and make them know that
if their love goes There, the Love they receive back is
Infinitely greater, and that Love from Above is the
Magnet that draws them out of the conditions that
form their distress and limitations in this World.

Now, why do you suppose I am thought of in
the physical world as a very Strong Being? Can you
imagine? Because the Power of the Great Central
Sun Magnet's Love is My Keynote to this World, to
be the Strength of Love in Life to draw the attention

away from the human discord, and be the Power to lift mankind into the Realm where Love rules All–Supreme! That is Power without limit!

Now, you are not supposed to love discord. Not at all! I want this thoroughly understood. But your love to Life, to your "Mighty I AM Presence" and the "Mighty I AM Presence" of all Life, your love to that Life is the Action of your Free Will, is the Gift–by your Free Will and your authority–from this outer self to the greater Life of your "Presence" and the Ascended Host, by which Their Love, Infinitely greater, can come down into your affairs and in and around you, and be the Protection and the Power that draws your conditions out of the control of destructive forces.

Your love to your "Mighty I AM Presence" and Our Great Octave of Life draws back to you Power that you cannot understand until you begin to qualify It and know It as the drawing Power of the Great Central Sun Magnet's Love. Then, as you teach yourself through your own experiences–or you allow your own "I AM Presence" to reveal to the outer self, through your own release of this Love–will you begin to understand what Power really is.

The Beloved Saint Germain told you that energy through use becomes Power. Energy becomes Power through use! Then, if you take the energy of the outer self and through love and devotion to your "I AM Presence" you give that love, you give the energy of your love to your "Presence," what do you think would be the Answer of your "Presence" to you? Wouldn't It shower you with more Love? Most certainly! Then Its Great Power of the Central Sun Magnet, Its Love flowing into the conditions of your world would, with Its Drawing Power, raise them into better and better and better conditions.

So will it be with you when you teach other people to love that "Mighty I AM Presence" and the Ascended Host. Just teach them to experiment with sending love to that which is greater than themselves, and let them experience for themselves what their love to the greater Life draws back to them as the greater Power to change their conditions into something that is Permanent Perfection.

Now, since I have the Strength and the Power of the Great Central Sun Magnet's Love to the Earth to release Power that mankind can scarcely comprehend, then I want you to understand that Power always, which I give through Radiation, as the Love from the Great Central Sun Magnet; for I give It to you from My Life and My Power of the Great Central Sun Magnet's Love, to be the Raising Power of My Life's Love to you, to lift you out of connection with that which has not been qualified with Love.

Therefore, when you have called forth the Invincible Honor Flame of God's Great Cosmic Heart
of Eternal Love, that is an Actual Flame that is drawn
forth from the Great Central Sun Magnet. That
Great Power of the Magnet as It pours Its Love to the
Earth to raise all into greater Power, then your love
to your "I AM Presence" and that Great Central Sun
Magnet—form the Raising Power of this World. And
you simply complete the circuit or the flow of that
Flame from your Heart's Life to that Life; and that
Life comes down here to this Life, and It lifts the substance and the energy of the outer world into the Perfection of Our Octave. You can't have the Perfection
of the Ascended Masters' Octave without the Understanding and Action of that Great Central Sun Magnet.

That is the reason the Beloved Master Jesus
gave you the Instruction of that Great Central Sun
Magnet, and said to you, "The more you use It, the
more will you understand It and the more will Its
Power act for you!"

People do not understand the Magnificent
Power and all the Blessings that can come to the
outer self by just pouring love to the "Mighty I AM
Presence" and the Ascended Host, and to the Great
Central Sun and to your Physical Sun! Can you
imagine wholly Perfect, Divine Beings of Cosmic

Life's Perfection not answering your love? If you give your love There, could there be such a condition that that "Presence" would not send Love back to you in Answer? Don't you consider it just an ordinary conventionality of life in this world, when someone does something for you, you say, "Thank you." You acknowledge that, do you not? Well, do you think We are any less polite than you are? If you sent Us your love, wouldn't We say, "Thank you," and give you Our Love back in return, when We are watching the Earth and rendering the Service that purifies it and raises it to luminosity! And that is another thing I want you to understand. If you want to make the flesh bodies luminous, then there must come your Call to your "Presence" and to the Great Central Sun Magnet's Love to reveal Itself through your flesh as Light, because that Love can produce any manifestation in this World—that is, any Quality that is producing Perfection.

     If you want that Light's Love to manifest in you as Strength and Power and Health and Courage, then that Love would come into you and make you feel those Qualities. If you want the flesh luminous, then that Love—you send your love first—then that Central Sun Magnet's Love, coming back into you, would manifest as Light! So do you not see, It contains all Qualities within Itself—all Power, all Supply, all Intelligence; and if you want It to manifest as Protection, It would produce and condense a Substance around you harder than steel. It might be invisible to the physical sight, but It would be so terrific in Its Concentrated Action that destruction could not come through.

Now, supposing you want to illumine the atmosphere about you. If you sent your love for that Manifestation to your "Presence" and to Us and to the Great Central Sun Magnet, and ask that the Great Central Sun Magnet's Love come down and around you in the atmosphere about you as Luminosity, It would soon begin to show in the atmosphere about you. Of course, I won't be responsible for the questions that would be asked you—not at all—if you do that! But you could also call to your "Blessed I AM Presence" through your love, and if questions were asked, ask your "Presence" to answer them!

You can understand anything in this Universe that is of God or God's Manifestation by sending your love through your attention to that which you want to understand, and ask the Great Central Sun Magnet's Love to draw that Understanding back into you. Then your "Beloved I AM Presence" has a clear, open Doorway through which to draw to you at any moment anything It might wish to use to give

you a Magnificent Experience in this World that
would bring you Joy for all Eternity.

Now, let us take one more thing; and I will not
hold you too long tonight. I want to give you a few
simple things that are so clear, you can never lose
them or never forget them.

The Healing which mankind requires needs to
be the Healing of that Love. Therefore, if you send
your love to the "Mighty I AM Presence" and the
Great Central Sun Magnet and ask that Its Love
come in and around you as the Healing Love of the
Universe, It would automatically just draw everything up and out of the vibratory action that is the
discord. It would change every vibration in and
around you, and would become the Purifying Flame
that releases the substance of the outer self from the
discord and impurity imposed upon it.

Now your Great Central Sun Magnet's Love is
absolutely imperative if you want to draw to yourselves Supply. You so often, you know, look to the
outer world and scratch around out here to get this
and that and something else. Poor, blessed humanity! The day you can get them to send their love to
their "Mighty I AM Presence" and the Ascended
Host, and ask the "Presence" to draw to them what
they require—just because they love the "Presence,"

there will not be such a thing as lack anywhere in this World.

When people want Supply from the outer world, if they would just first love the "Presence"—turn away from the need and give that "Presence" some love, and *call to the Great Central Sun Magnet to release the Love that draws the things, if things you require, of this world into your outer use harmoniously, to produce Perfection for you and never bring with them one problem.*

Don't you think I am strong? And I am strong for the Understanding of that Love, and I am determined to use all the Power of Creation, if need be, to bring This before the attention of mankind until they believe Me enough to at least experiment with It until I can prove to them, by their own use of It, the Magnificence of Its Power and the Eternal Law of Its Action.

So, the next time you need anything in the physical world, whether it be money or things or friends or opportunities, before you even look to the outer world for them, won't you just send your love to your "Presence" and then to the Great Central Sun Magnet, and ask It to pour Its Love down and around you and draw to you That which fulfills the Requirements, fulfills the Divine Plan, and leaves in your world more Love than you will ever require again!

The day mankind are taught to draw—to give love first to the "Mighty I AM Presence" and the Great Host, and then draw Love into this World to solve these problems, there cannot live longer the hordes of darkness; and they are dark because they lack that Love.

That which is here must someday become purified and made self-luminous once again. And the Love from the Great Central Sun Magnet is the only Power that can do it. That Love is your Violet Consuming Flame. That Love is the Great Creative Word "I AM"! That Love is your own Heart's Flame. That Love is your Higher Mental Body. That Love is your "Electronic Presence." That Love is all the Substance of Light in the Universe; and that Love is Power Supreme. That Love is God's Eternal Victory, which you have used in your Decree tonight. Keep it up, knowing It as the Love from the Great Central Sun Magnet, Its Power of Love, when you give those Decrees; and see for yourselves whether your Answer is instantaneous and eternal. It may take a little bit of time at first before it reaches that quick response; and yet, if you send the feeling intense enough, the response will be instantaneous.

Dear Ones, the Joy is so great when you know you have all Power, all Freedom, and all Authority to give that Love; and then know the Power of the

Great Central Sun Magnet's Love flows into the conditions of this World, and you stand and observe
those conditions changed in answer to your Call.
Many times you don't even have to do a thing!
Events of life will automatically change those conditions for you harmoniously, permanently; and then
your changed conditions will never bring you another
problem.

Your obligation to your "Presence" and to the
Life of the universe around you is to give that love
first.   Your obligation to your fellowman in this
World is to teach all Life to love the Source of Life
that gives them existence, and to love the Central
Source that produces manifestation.

So, may the Strength of My Heart's Love ever
abide within and around you as God's Eternal Victory for which you have called. And when you think
of Me, instead of thinking of Me as someone with
strong muscles, I would rather you would think of
Me as one whose Heart's Flame is strong with Love
to Life that can never be exhausted, that loves to
love, and loves to give of Itself to bring everything
into the Great Joy of the Eternal Victory of God's
Perfection in the Ascended Masters' Octave; and to
dissolve and consume in this World everything that is
not the Love of Eternal Light, the Love of Eternal
Perfection.

So Precious Ones, when you want My Herculean Protection, it is tantamount to saying you want My Herculean Love to stand between you and the destruction of the outer world; and if you ask for My Love, you shall always receive It! I have never once ever refused It to any part of Life. And so shall you, one day, know the Glory of Its Power by using the Great Central Sun Magnet's Love. When you think you need things of this World, when imperfection appears, you will call that Power into action, and you will forever remain untouched by the destructive forces of this World. You have nothing to fear from tonight.

Send your love to your "Presence" and to Us, to that Great Central Sun Magnet; and that Love is Master over this World! If you ask for that Central Sun Magnet's Love to come in and through and around you as your Deliverer come, hate cannot approach, hate cannot live within, hate cannot manifest in your world; and there is nothing so Supreme as that Love which is your own "Precious I AM Presence" and the Life of the Great Central Sun, the Life of the Ascended Masters in Their Great Octave of Beauty and Perfection. And that Love, that Power, that Life is Freedom!

May It clothe you tonight with the ever-present reminder that the Great Central Sun Magnet's Love, ever pouring back in answer to you, is your Solution

for every problem in this World. Try Me out, and
let us go forward and teach Life everywhere to love
the Great Source, the "Mighty I AM Presence," that
gives us all.

Thank you with that Love tonight.

(Record SG 1927)

Excerpt on Beloved Hercules' Sevenfold Blue Flame

Beloved Hercules

There is something else I wish to bring to your attention and show you how far down through the centuries has come some recognition of Me. The thought of Hercules as the giant of Power has not died in the minds of men. They have portrayed Me rather amusingly sometimes. I do not look like some of the pictures they have drawn–thank Heaven; but that was *their idea* in those pictures, not My Appearance. I hope before too long, you may have My Likeness and I trust I will not disappoint you, or the picture will not. It represents some of My Activities with the Fire Element. . . .

Each one of the Seven Mighty Elohim has a definite Service to perform naturally to the Earth, yet each one uses Unlimited Power, Unlimited Energy. Each one has all the Qualities of each other, but one is paramount; for each one is a special Service which that Life Stream offers. So as the Elohim of Peace said to you that the Power of Peace is necessary in the outer, so do I say to you in every constructive quality that you call forth, you must have some action of the Blue Ray within it or you don't have any energy to make it act. . . .

GREAT HERCULES ☙ ~THOU ELOHIM

If you will call for My Sevenfold Blue Flame to strengthen every quality within you that is constructive and to protect every quality that is constructive, then I will be able to bless you more powerfully than ever before. Remember, a direct Flame from My Heart is anchored within the forehead of every human being on this Earth, and through that Flame I have given you from the beginning the Blessings of My Life Stream.

("Voice of the I AM," October 1944)

CHAPTER XII
Beloved Elohim Hercules

Chicago, Illinois
June 26, 1970

Beloved of Our Hearts, I trust I may bring to you tonight something of the Inner Explanation of what Our Service to each one of your Life Streams means, how We bring It about, how you can have more of Its Power in outer use, and how you can use It to help all that you contact everywhere you go.

Our Life Streams have placed a Flame of Our Love in your foreheads. Therefore, the Sevenfold Flame of the Seven Mighty Elohim is definitely for your use, and is definitely located within the physical structure of your flesh bodies. It is My whole Protection around your own Life Stream, Our own Hearts' Flame, and also gives to you Our Protecting Love to enfold whatever your "Presence" wants to do through you in the Protection that gives you Our Victory, the Victory of your "Mighty I AM Presence," the Victory of the Great Central Sun, the Victory of the Ascended Masters' Octave.

So when you feel sometimes that conditions in the physical world seem overwhelming to you, don't let that come in and cause a depression within you or cause you to be worried, or get under an emotional strain or under a nervous tension or under any activity of fear, if you can possibly avoid it.

The reason I ask this is because if the moment you are aware of mistakes or problems, or something that is of destruction in the outer world trying to interfere with what you wish to accomplish, don't stop and argue with it! Don't stop and argue with yourself. The moment you are aware of any feeling of opposition or discord or strain or struggle, *stop just a moment, and pouring the love from your own Heart Flame to your "Beloved I AM Presence"—and as you do that, feel that your Heart Flame, as It expands, becomes One with the Sevenfold Flame of the Seven Mighty Elohim in your forehead, and then reaches up to make the Call to your "Presence."*

As soon as you do that, then *call for the Herculean Blazing Sacred Fire of Our Elohim Love into yourselves first, to give you Peace and make you feel Our Control of the physical conditions,* because Our Flash of Flame can control things in an instant that you on the physical side cannot control. Therefore, when discord needs to be consumed or repelled from conditions in which you are either active, or you wish to bring forth something constructive, don't wait and give the sinister force a chance to come in and strike fear or doubt or any activity of the human outer world feeling that is everywhere in the rest of mankind.

If you will learn to handle every feeling of which you are aware, the moment any discord comes within you, don't wait and go on and struggle under it when in one or two Calls to your "Beloved Mighty I AM Presence"—and as you make the Call to Us, whenever you say, "Beloved Mighty I AM Presence," at the same time feel the Unfed Flame in your Heart expand and reach up to the Sevenfold Flame of the Seven Mighty Elohim, and again reach up and enfold your "Presence." As that becomes a habit of the Expansion of your own Heart's Flame joined with Ours to reach up to your "Mighty I AM Presence" in your Call, then *call for whatever Elohim Sacred Fire Love We know handles the situation, changes the feeling within you, consumes what is wrong, repels what is wrong, keeps your attention on Our Mastery and Our Release of the Sacred Fire of Our Love, Our Sacred Fire Love into the condition, that harmonizes the atmosphere about you!*

Then your "Mighty I AM Presence" can direct you more clearly. You will receive the Direction without mistakes or distortion; and at the same time Our Sacred Fire Love will hold around you the Peace and the Harmony and Protection that you need in order to be steady and receive from your "Presence" whatever will fulfill the Divine Plan, and whatever Power It wishes to release through you to handle conditions in the outer world that are sometimes very disturbing, sometimes quite disastrous, and sometimes only impose upon you more and more problems.

This will do a great deal to help you handle conditions easily in the outer world; and as you use It more and more, It will prevent mistakes and prevent those problems coming into you or your world, because the more you can think about the Unfed Flame in your Heart and feel It expand and become *One* with the Sevenfold Flame in the forehead, and again expand and carry your love to your "Mighty I AM Presence" in your Call, then when you ask for My Herculean Love, My Sacred Fire Herculean Love to blaze into you Its Peace and My Herculean Feeling of Mastery, fear and doubt and selfishness that are the suggestions in the outer world will not be able to qualify your energy within yourself. Therefore, it will stay at a distance and either be repelled or consumed.

Then when you ask for My Heart's Flame to charge into a condition whatever I know consumes it, you'll give Me an Opportunity to release more Power around you. And every time I do that, more of My Heart Flame will come within you and become

One with your own Heart's Flame. As It expands to fill the outer self, We will hold you at Peace in the midst of outer world conditions, if you will only let Our Sacred Fire Love come in and fill you with Our Mastery. Every Wave of Love We send is Master over everything within you and through you and around you if you will let It come through. But you must ask for It; and you must call and release into yourselves first Our Sacred Fire Love, because you love to.

When the love in your own Heart reaches up to Our Elohim Love, recognizes Our Presence within your own Life, and then again pours love to your "Mighty I AM Presence," you give Us a Threefold Activity of the Sacred Fire from the Ascended Masters' Octave that We can project into any condition and change it, if it be discordant, into that which fulfills the Divine Plan. This will prevent you becoming exhausted. It will prevent you becoming the victims of the fear suggestions in the outer world, because they are everywhere.

Mankind is generating so much destruction all the time, fear is so rampant everywhere, that if you don't keep yourself insulated from it, it will come in and destroy you, just like it will destroy anything else in the outer world. But when you fill yourselves with Our Sacred Fire Control of Manifestation, when you

ask Us to fill you with what We know makes you not
only Master over, but keeps out of you the fear of the
outer world and the selfishness of the outer world,
you will give your own "Beloved I AM Presence"
Unconditional Freedom through the outer self to release Perfection into you and through you and into
your affairs; and you will not go on and feel the exhaustion or the fear and the destruction that, many
times, make you make mistakes and but create more
problems.

When, sometimes in the outer world you think
you know what to do to solve a problem, if you do
not know all that is there, you can open yourselves
and temporarily solve a problem and with it you will
draw several other problems, perhaps greater than
the one you're trying to solve; and This will prevent
that.

Now mankind does not understand who the
Seven Mighty Elohim are, and what Power of Love
We wield to control all manifestation. That is why
We are called the Seven Powers around the Throne,
the Seven Builders around the Throne, because We
are definitely concerned with the Control of Manifestation in this physical world; and We concern Ourselves with it, first of all, within your own physical
bodies, within your own minds, within your feeling,

and then within your atmosphere, then into the conditions that you have to handle in the physical world.

So if you want more help in the outer world to bring to you the conditions that fulfill the Divine Plan and enable you to do something constructive to help others, please give Us the Opening to pour into you, first, Our own Hearts' Love, the Sacred Fire Love of the Seven Mighty Elohim that builds and builds and builds and will always build Perfection in you, through you, around you, and anywhere you call It into outer activity. You can send It to others, just the same as you can send a thought or a telegram or a message, or can talk over a telephone. You have no doubt about your message reaching the person that you want, when you use outer world means of communication. Very many times you do not always get through when you want to, because there is obstruction in the outer world. But there is no obstruction to Us! I want you to realize this tonight. That's why We are Master over the physical world.

There isn't a condition you have in your world today that Our Sacred Fire can't move into and consume it on the instant. That is why, if you will recognize that within your own Heart Flame is the Love from the Great Central Sun that gives you existence, It is you, the Being, who made the choice to come into physical existence.

I want you to become acquainted with the Unfed Flame in your own Heart, because most people
don't know they have one. They know something
about the Heart when they have Heart trouble, or
they think they do; but mankind does not understand
that within the physical Heart itself there is a Flame
from the "Mighty I AM Presence" from the Great
Central Sun. It abides within your Inner Bodies; and
if you will recognize This every time you want anything constructive, if you'll remember the part in you
that wants something constructive, the Desire in you
for something constructive is the Desire within your
own Heart, the Great Central Sun's Desire for you to
have Perfection, to expand It, to give It to the rest of
the Universe, and to let It control manifestation
wherever you abide, because It is the Master Power
of the Universe.

Therefore, whenever you need help in the outer
world, please remember Our Existence. And turning
your attention, first of all recognize the Unfed Flame
in your Heart, which is the Sacred Fire, and as It
reaches up and becomes *One* with the Sevenfold
Flame of the Seven Mighty Elohim and again expands Its Love to the "Mighty I AM Presence," your
Higher Mental Body and your "Electronic Presence"
and your Causal Body—just reach your Flame up
There and ask the Seven Mighty Elohim to blaze in

and around you what We know makes you Our
Mastery over everything in this World. Your own
"Beloved I AM Presence" can fill you with Its Master
Powers, pour Them through you, control conditions
around you; and We hold the Protection and furnish
the Sacred Fire Love that sometimes you yourself
cannot furnish in the outer world because there is battle between personalities.

    We can furnish enough Sacred Fire Love in and
around your own Life Stream to control conditions
around you, that your own "Mighty I AM Presence"
may exert Its Mastery and produce out here what
fulfills the Divine Plan. If people would only understand This and use It, they just would not make mistakes and would not create problems. Now you'll
have activity, plenty of it, but you won't have the discord; and the only one Divine Way to live Life anywhere in this World or any other anywhere in infinite
space, the only way that you have to live Life the
harmonious way, the constructive way to fulfill the
Divine Plan, is to be continuously aware that the Sacred Fire Love in your Life Stream is the Heart of the
Universe, as well as within your physical Heart.

    Now when mankind understands what the Sa-
cred Fire is and begins to use It, We won't have to do
any more explaining about the Inner Action of the
Law because This will teach you of Itself, because It

will illumine the brain structure. It will consume the
human concepts that have been the misunderstanding
that has made the mistakes.

When you call Our Sacred Fire of the Seven
Mighty Elohim, Our Consciousness of that Sacred
Fire Love into yourselves, you won't have any concepts in the mind that are wrong. It will prevent mistakes. It will prevent problems and let your "Mighty
I AM Presence" have Command of the outer self;
and what you call "work" today will simply be a joyous activity, and the struggle will be but a memory.
We hope you don't remember it very long; and if
you use Our Sacred Fire Love, you won't! *(applause)*
Thank you so much. Won't you be seated, please.

We want to train a certain number of mankind
to live in this World while it is yet discordant. We
want to train a certain number of Life Streams to
bring Perfection into this World in the midst of its
chaos, and make your Perfection Invincible against
the chaos. And that Mastery comes only from the
Sacred Fire! It doesn't come from anywhere else. It
comes from the Sacred Fire in your Heart, comes
from the Sacred Fire of the Seven Mighty Elohim,
comes from the Sacred Fire of your Higher Mental
Body and your "Electronic Presence," comes from
the Sacred Fire in the Causal Body, comes from the

Sacred Fire in the Physical Sun and the Great Central Sun.

Therefore, if We can have a group of people who will establish this habit, We can bring such Perfection in and around you as to make you Victorious over everything in the outer world. And do you know why? We want you to obey the Law and fulfill the Divine Plan as completely for your own Life Stream, as a flower does in the outer world's chaos and destruction.

If you analyze, many times, the activity of the Powers of Nature and Forces of the Elements, the Life that controls and expands Beauty and Perfection and Blessings through the Powers of Nature and Forces of the Elements, those blessed, blessed plants go on and fulfill their own Divine Plan, no matter what surrounds them. This is what We would like to experiment with and express through you, in order to make you Invincible against the discord and failure and destruction and filth of the world around you. We want you to go on and manifest the Fulfillment of your Divine Plan while yet the outer world's chaos still exists; and then you can make the Call to help consume the discord in the outer world, because you will be Master over it. There is only one Mastery in all Creation, and It's the Sacred Fire Love's Eternal Purity from the Ascended Masters' Octave, as well as your own "Beloved Mighty I AM Presence" and Higher Mental Body.

I want you to feel that Our Presence is so near, so powerfully within you, that you do not fear the conditions of the outer world, and you don't doubt, ever, the Answers to your Calls. You don't doubt your "Presence" or the Ascended Host. Your doubt is the thing that locks the Door and doesn't let the Sacred Fire Love come and produce the Perfection!

Anytime you let Sacred Fire Love from your "Mighty I AM Presence" and Higher Mental Body, or from the Sevenfold Flame of the Seven Mighty Elohim, come into you or around you, or from any Ascended Master's Heart Flame to whom you call, the moment you let that Sacred Fire Love come into you and you begin to feel It, let It pour forth Its Radiation—while you are feeling It, ask It to be made Eternal in your flesh, and see whether We mean business or not! See whether We can transmute your outer troubles into your Peace and Perfection of the Divine Plan fulfilled.

This is the Master Power of the Universe and is the only Mastery there is. It's the Source of Perfection. It never can be contaminated; and It's the only Victory in all creation that is Master over mankind's frightful evil.

Now the reason I am calling This to your attention, and the reason I am accepted, so to speak, by outer world consciousness as a Being of such Force or Power, Herculean Power, is because I do direct that Cosmic Electronic Force from the Great Central Sun that is Boundless and Overwhelming to everything in manifestation. But when you realize that My Power of that Electronic Force is My Sacred Fire Love from the Great Central Sun, and I offer That to come into you, and ask you to let Us fill you with It in order to prevent what is wrong, and blazing through you to help the world around you, you have but to fill yourselves with Our Sacred Fire Love. And when you call forth My Herculean Power of that Sacred Fire, It can be the Herculean Power of Purity and Peace and Indestructible Harmony, and such Invincible Victory no human creation can interfere with It.

That is what I want you to accept in order to make you Invincible against the selfishness, the doubt, the fear, and the destructive forces of the outer world; and if you don't fill yourselves with the Sacred Fire's Indestructible, Herculean Purity of that Love, then the outer world's going to fill you with its discord.

You don't have to stay in discord! You don't have to stay in limitations! You don't have to be filled with fear and doubt and selfishness! We can get rid of all of it, inside of you, if you want Us to! *(applause)* Thank you so much.

Now, Beloved Ones, the mankind's discord in this World was never originally designed, never God created, never was and never will be part of the original Divine Plan! It doesn't have to be in existence now. You don't have to put up with it! If you want to fill yourselves and the world around you with My Herculean Love of the Sacred Fire's Indestructible Purity, the Sacred Fire's Indestructible Victory and Mastery over all Creation, My Sacred Fire All-Protecting Perfection of Existence, I can flash that Flame; and all mankind put together can't put It out! *(applause)* Thank you so much.

All mankind's discord put together can't put Me out of this World, and My Retreat is within the United States of America. There is a Flame there that all mankind on Earth can never change or interfere with. This is part of the Protection of your Nation, and your Nation is the Protection of the Heart of the World. There is only one Protection of Eternity, and It is the Great Central Sun's Sacred Fire Love Protecting Perfection of Eternity, forever expanding.

So if We may experiment with you—not that We doubt the results, not at all; We know what We can do! We know what Our Sacred Fire Love can do! We know what Power We can release; and We

know what mankind has to bow to when We care to
use the Herculean Sacred Fire Power of the Seven
Mighty Elohim of Creation. All mankind put together aren't masters over That! This World has to
be purified and re-ordered in order to survive. Destructive forces won't save this Nation or this World;
and destructive forces won't save you, and they won't
solve your problems. They won't take you out of the
clutches of the beast, and they won't take the beast
out of the World. But *by God We will,* if you will call!
(applause) By the God Flame of the Universe, the Great
Central Sun Heart Flame, *by the God Flame* of the
Seven Mighty Elohim of Creation in the forehead of
every Life Stream on this Earth, We can expand that
Sacred Fire to consume everything of discord mankind has created; and This must come if your Nation
is to survive and Peace be established in the World
for the Ascension of all.

The destructive forces of mankind won't give
anyone the Ascension; and there is no freedom from
the world of imperfection and limitation until you
gain the Ascension. And the only thing in the Universe that can give you the Ascension is the Sacred
Fire Love in your own Heart Flame, the Sacred Fire
Love of the Seven Mighty Elohim in your brain
structure, the Sacred Fire Love of your "Mighty

I AM Presence" and the Great Central Sun and the
Ascended Masters' Octave of Light.

I am determined, with your cooperation, to
bring the Cosmic Illumination, and I mean Herculean
Illumination of the Fiery Christ Truth of what the
Sacred Fire Love of the Seven Mighty Elohim has
done for mankind all down through the centuries,
and which must come into outer world action if mankind's destruction is to cease; and I assure you, it is to
cease, no matter whose it is! *(applause)* Thank you so
much.

Now, Blessed Ones, if you'll remember Me as
the Power, the Sacred Fire Power and Electronic
Force of the Sacred Fire Love of the Seven Mighty
Elohim and the Great Central Sun, and as your
Guarding Presence of your intellect, the Guarding
Presence of your physical structure of the brain, Our
Love, Sacred Fire Love, is the Guarding Presence of
your own Heart's Flame within your physical flesh
body. Now, just because the medical world can't dig
out Our Flame and put It in a laboratory somewhere,
doesn't mean We are not in existence.

Somebody is going to learn something besides
what the physical sight at the present time can behold; and I want you to use This for the sake of prov-
ing to yourself that there is a Flame in your Heart.
You know there's Life in your Heart that beats it, but

you don't know that that Flame is there until you see It. And I hope every one of you has the same experience this Messenger had when she saw that Flame come forth at least a foot in extent, six to eight inches wide; and It was there for twenty minutes to half an hour, on a streetcar in broad daylight when she was thoroughly awake. I want you to have that, because you won't know completely what It is till you see It and have It within yourself, and you watch It expand. Then you know what you are! You are That! I want you to have that experience, because It's Harmonious. It is Constructive! It is Illumining! It is Victorious! It is the Perfection of Life, and every human being in existence can have It; and I want you to see the Sevenfold Flame of the Seven Mighty Elohim in your own brain structure as well.

The day you realize that the Inner Activities of your Life are the Sacred Fire Love and Purity of Eternity, and are Indestructible, you won't fear anything in this World. You will know you are That; and *That's the Master Presence of all Creation!*

We have guarded your Life Streams, Beloved Ones, in every embodiment you have ever had! You've had sometimes hundreds and sometimes thousands of embodiments; and We have come and enfolded your Life Stream hundreds and thousands of times, in order to make you aware of all that the

Sacred Fire Power and Love of Life is in the Universe, and that you can use, and that you must use in this World to produce the Manifestation of the Perfection that is the Divine Plan fulfilled, because Perfection is the Destiny of Life, and is the only thing mankind should ever have experienced.

There are Limitless Legions of the Angels of that Perfection of that Sacred Fire! There are limitless Worlds and Systems of Worlds that have never had any discord on them! Every part of manifestation doesn't have to go through the discord and the filth and the destruction that this World has experienced in order to fulfill the Great Infinite Plan in the Scheme of Creation.

I want you to understand what the Sacred Fire is, and if you'll experiment with This, the Sevenfold Flame of the Seven Mighty Elohim will teach you; and you will become that Fulfillment of that Divine Plan. You will become the Victory of the Sacred Fire's Almighty Control of all Manifestation in existence; and it seems to Me, that is a very much more comfortable way to live than your present existence.

We don't suffer! We don't have limitation! We never lack for any good thing! We're afraid of nothing! Nothing can make Us fear! Nothing can undo anything We do, so wouldn't you like Our Mastery? I think so! *(applause)* Thank you so much.

There is only one thing that is Master of everything in manifestation, from the Great Central Sun to
everything in existence in this World or any other;
and It is the Great Central Sun's Heart Flame. It is
the Sevenfold Flame of the Seven Mighty Elohim;
and if you want Our Presence with you, We will be
with you. And any time you open the Door, Our
Flame will come; but there has to come Conscious
Awareness, Understanding, Recognition, and Use of
Our Sacred Fire Love inside of yourself, to protect
and expand your own Heart's Flame, and then to
clear the way, so your own "Blessed Mighty I AM
Presence" and Higher Mental Body can pour Its own
Sacred Fire through you, reveal Its Perfection, fulfill
the Divine Plan, produce constructive activity in the
outer world, and give that Perfection to the world
around you, like the Sun gives light to the Earth.
There isn't anything in this World or any other as a
Way and Means of producing manifestation and controlling it, and raising all Life into greater and greater
Perfection, except by this Conscious Recognition of
the Sacred Fire which "I AM".

That is why the Blessed Mighty Saint Germain
brought forth this Knowledge of the "Mighty I AM
Presence," because when the Desire within you says,
"I AM that I AM", and you acknowledge that *That* is
the Eternal You, That is your *Eternal Identity*, That is

the Master Presence of all infinite space and all manifestation forever, then you give Us the Opening.
And then when you say, *"'I AM' the Sevenfold Flame of
the Seven Mighty Elohim's Love in outer physical use in everything I do; and wherever I am, It lights my way, perfects all
things. And wherever I go, 'I AM' Victory! 'I AM' Protecting Perfection! 'I AM' the Purifying Love and Peace that is
the Divine Plan, and the Divine Plan's Fulfillment of the Ascension of every particle of Life in this World or any other, the
rest of Eternity!"*—when people don't want That, they
don't know what they want or don't want. When
people don't want the Perfection of Love and Peace
and Eternal Protection and Mastery, then the sinister
force has only one answer; and people can take it or
leave it.

We have consumed and consumed and consumed mankind's frightful filth and misuse of Life's
energy and consciousness, age after age after age in
this World; and people should be taught a better way
to live Life than to chase their own desires that don't
do anything but destroy them. If you let the Desire in
the Unfed Flame in your Heart reach up and love the
Sevenfold Flame of the Seven Mighty Elohim, and
reach up again and love the "Mighty I AM Presence"
and the Ascended Host, reach up again and enfold
the Ascended Masters and Cosmic Beings in the love
from your own Heart's Flame, you will find there will

come back into you Our Sacred Fire Love, and That of your Higher Mental Body and "Electronic Presence," that will fill you with the Desire of the Perfection of Life that is Invincible and is Eternal Mastery.

So Blessed Ones, you can shock mankind awake by the Use of this Sacred Fire Love from the Heart Flame of the Seven Mighty Elohim of Creation; and mankind needs to be shocked awake in order to take it out of the clutches of the destruction of its own human creation. When people don't want greater Perfection and don't want the rest of Life to be free from suffering, then it is time that the individual be shocked awake by some Manifestations of the Sacred Fire that nobody is going to oppose.

Now I come to something that the outer world doesn't understand, except in a very hazy way as certain activities have come down through the historical events of time. What do you think would be the reaction of a group of people of the outer world if I were to suddenly come, or any one of the Seven Mighty Elohim—where We stand fourteen, fifteen feet high—and We would just suddenly manifest and control a group of people, what do you think would be the reaction of the human creation in those individuals? Fear! And when that fear is released by the Light in an individual, and that Life bound in the outer self in discord fears the Love and the Light of

Eternal Perfection, where do you suppose Victory is? Where do you suppose the Fulfillment of the Divine Plan is? What do you suppose is the Destiny of Life when people fear that which is of Love—what hope is there for them until they are purified?

That is why the Mighty Saint Germain gave the use of the Violet Consuming Flame; and the Elohim of the Violet Consuming Flame governs the Violet Flame to this World, and is the Violet Flame Heaven on Earth to which you have called, and of which the Mighty Saint Germain is Master, and in which you cannot feel any discord. Wouldn't it be a relief to go somewhere where you couldn't feel any distress? Wouldn't that be at least variety from what you are experiencing? I think so!

So, if you'll begin to experiment with filling yourselves with My Herculean Heart Flame's Sacred Fire Love's Purifying Peace and All-Protecting Perfection, inside of you, that I know makes you Victorious within and around, when you begin to experiment with that, you will give Me an Opening to increase It in and around you. And your "Beloved I AM Presence" will be Grateful for Eternity that you will let It expand Perfection through you, fulfill the Divine Plan, and help the rest of Life to Ascend as you gain your own.

Blessed Ones, there is no failure! There is nothing that can't be accomplished by that Sacred Fire which We direct. Mankind needs to become acquainted with It and know what It wants, and know that every Life Stream in existence can call It forth within the outer self, can use It, can expand Its Perfection through the outer self, can give It to the rest of Life; and wherever That comes, discord cannot be! That ought to be a relief to mankind's present way of Life!

From tonight, if you'll feel Me closer and closer within and around yourselves, you will give Me an Opportunity to call forth the Elohim Angels; and you'll find the Star Angels are very Real, Tangible Beings, whose Perfection and Power are Indescribable. Only as you see Them and feel Their Love, and feel Them control physical conditions around you, only as you see that, can you realize how *Great* They are; and I want you to become acquainted with Them. If the outer world doesn't believe it, that's just too bad. That's the outer world's mistake, that's all. We have these Blessings to give! They're in the Universe. They are the Divine Plan fulfilled, and mankind cannot get Free without Them.

The Blessed Jesus and the Beloved Mary came! They took away the hate and the doubt and the fear from a certain proportion of mankind, in order to

leave in the atmosphere of Earth the Record of the
Destiny of Life, and the Attainment that each Life
Stream could reach up and enter into, for Freedom
from discord.

Beloved Master Jesus set that Eternal Etheric
Record! Beloved Saint Germain gave the Violet
Consuming Flame to purify the human creation that
enslaves mankind to the second death. And I come
to bring the Herculean Love that can clear the way
inside of you and, if you will use It, clear the way
through you and around you and let your own
"Beloved I AM Presence" pour forth into you Its Victory of Eternity, until there blazes through you everything that gives you the Ascension, because It has
consumed everything that is of limitation or delay. In
your own Victory you can offer that same Assistance
to the rest of Life; and when you don't want the rest
of Life to be Free, you'll be bound in distress until
you do, because you can't have Freedom unless you
give It! You can't have Love unless you give It! You
can't have the Fulfillment of the Divine Plan unless
you help to fulfill that Divine Plan for the rest of Life.

Our Use of the Sevenfold Flame of the Seven
Mighty Elohim, and Our Love from the Great Central Sun, is the only Way and Means Life provides
for the mankind who embody in this World to be purified and raised, and fulfill the Divine Plan to enter

into the Ascended Masters' Octave, and leave the
mistakes of human creation forever consumed in this
World; and the World, purified, becomes filled with
the Ascended Masters' Perfection of Eternity.   Only
the Sacred Fire Love can fill it with that Perfection.

Blessed Ones, I simply offer It to you tonight
for your use if you will call It into outer physical conditions; but first of all, fill yourselves with It, because
you must become It.   Then give It to the rest of Life;
and you will find your pathway illumined and clear,
and the Fulfillment of the Divine Plan will bring
Blessings to you and the rest of Life wherever you go,
and you are not longer held in the distress of outer
world conditions.

I commend you to That which the Mighty Saint
Germain has opened the Door for you to have by the
use of the Violet Consuming Flame, to consume everything that is a barrier between Our Sacred Fire
Love and the love in your own Heart, and the Sacred
Fire Love of your "Mighty I AM Presence"; and if
you will let It come through, you can be at Peace.
You can give that Peace to others; and wherever you
go, Purity takes the place of mankind's evil.   I hope
you want to be a part of Our Victory and Mastery
over everything in this World that is not the Ascended Masters' Way of Life for Eternity.

I clothe you in the Miracle Mantle of My Sacred Fire Love of the Seven Mighty Elohim; and may It hold you in Its Heart and make you feel Its Peace for Eternity; and Power without limit is then yours to use in outer world conditions, till your Victory is everywhere forever! Thank you with all My Heart.

(Record CD 1621)

CHAPTER XIII
Beloved Elohim Orion

Chicago, Illinois
December 1, 1968

Beloved Ones of the Mighty Saint Germain's Family, We come this hour to give you Assistance that only Love can give; and the Love to which We refer is now drawing into this World the Pressure of the All-Controlling Powers of this System of Worlds, to keep Balance and Divine Law and Order in Control of the Powers of Nature and Forces of the Elements.

For your own Protection, We ask you to draw forth sometime each day the All-Purifying, All-Protecting Love of your "Beloved I AM Presence," and then of the Seven Mighty Elohim of Creation, and then of all the Ascended Masters and Cosmic Beings who govern the Powers of Nature and Forces of the Elements. In this way, if sometime every day you charge forth the Sacred Fire's All-Purifying Love from the Ascended Masters' Octave into all the Powers of Nature and Forces of the Elements, with the Command that they be released from all impurity and destruction mankind has imposed upon them, you will find them becoming your Guardians, as well as your Suppliers for many of the things that you need and use in your physical, everyday life.

The Powers of Nature and Forces of the Elements have served you a very long time; and they've given you many, many Blessings, just countless Blessings by which you have had the opportunity to do what you wanted to do. But they are entitled to love from your Life Streams now, to release them from the impurity and destruction mankind has imposed upon them, not only through war, but down through the centuries in the misuse of the Blessings of the Powers of Nature and Forces of the Elements.

But in order to avoid a focus of destructive activity, form the habit of asking your "Beloved I AM Presence" and all of Us who govern the Powers of Nature and Forces of the Elements, to dissolve and consume everywhere as quickly as possible, all impurity and discord imposed upon them, and make them your Ascended Master Friends.

As you call This forth to release them from the discord and impurity of mankind's creation, you will find them very, very grateful to you for removing the discord, because, I assure you, the Intelligent Beings in the Powers of Nature and Forces of the Elements respond very quickly to any love that is poured to them by mankind.

So, as you call forth the Blessing of your own "Beloved I AM Presence" and That from the Ascended Masters' Octave, to release the Powers of Nature and Forces of the Elements from all discord and all impurity, it will have a double effect. It will have a very wonderful, purifying effect upon your own physical bodies. It will help to purify your flesh, the atmosphere about you. It will help to purify your emotional bodies, your feeling world. It ever comes back to you as very great Love and Gratitude and Blessings by those Beings who, I assure you, are Intelligent Beings—otherwise they could not create the magnificent beauty and perfection of the flower kingdom, the food that is produced for mankind's sustaining, and all the many, many Blessings they give to mankind all the time.

But because they are Intelligent Beings, they are entitled to the Purity and the Love which is the great God Perfection of the Universe. And when they have served you so well and so long, it will be a very great Blessing to you if you, sometime each day, make the Call to your "Beloved I AM Presence" and to Us, to release all the Sacred Fire of Our Purifying Love to free the Powers of Nature and Forces of the Elements from all discord and impurity imposed on them by mankind. In doing this, you will find a very great relief coming into your own feeling world, and it will be a sense of Freedom you have never known before.

This is very vital for your own safety, because then if you have been in the habit of pouring forth your love and blessings to them and calling forth their Purity and Perfection, there abides within you the same great Activity of the Sacred Fire; and wherever you go, that is a Magnet to attract their constructive activities to protect you and to supply you and to cooperate with you in anything you want to do, so long as it be constructive.

So Blessed Ones, there are many, many, many Blessings that can come to you if you will do this; and when all is said and done, the Blessings of the Powers of Nature and Forces of the Elements are Infinite, and can be made Eternal wherever you abide.

Therefore, We would appreciate this very, very greatly for your Protection, as well as the Protection of the structure of Earth itself, or your Nation or the World. And in doing this, you will also find a very great Peace coming into you, and much of your struggle, much of the resistance you have felt in doing outer world physical things, you will find just removed; and your effort to do things in the physical world will be much less, and it will produce very much greater Perfection for you.   It will remove much of your struggle.   It will enable you to live very much more comfortably, very much more safely, and very much more Invincibly Victorious in accomplishing the things you wish to do that are constructive, and therefore are the Fulfillment of the Great Divine Plan.

In the Power that We want to draw into outer physical conditions that comes forth from the Great Central Sun, It is a Pressure of Energy from the Great Central Sun.   And as the Sacred Fire blazes It into the physical substance of this World and into the atmosphere of the World, It is a Powerful Purifying Activity, and is the Eternal Re-establishing of the Balance of the Forces of the Elements and the Powers of Nature, to readjust much of the conditions in the physical world that have been thrown out of balance by mankind's discord and will go on and continue to destroy many, many things if this Help is not given.

When We come to release the Cosmic Sacred Fire from the Great Central Sun of Our Love into the physical octave, It is to hold certain forces in Balanced Action.   And when We pour that Sacred Fire Love and release Its Pressure, It re-establishes the Balance that was here in the former Golden Ages, was here in the beginning, and that must now return here.   But mankind must do something to call forth

Purity into the Powers of Nature and Forces of the Elements, because human beings in their use of the energy and substance of this World have imposed upon it so much that is destructive, that now it is about to return upon mankind unless some Help of this sort is given.

If you will just make it a habit to call forth sometime each day whatever We know—and I mean the Seven Mighty Elohim and all the Ascended Masters and Cosmic Beings—what We know will purify the Powers of Nature and Forces of the Elements wherever you abide, It will not only purify the conditions of the outer world, but that Purification will go on within your own physical flesh. It will go on in your mental and feeling world. It will go on in your own atmosphere. Sometime every day as you'd call It forth to all the Powers of Nature and Forces of the Elements, a certain amount of That must come within you and give you Its Blessing, as you are willing to bless those activities of life of the outer world that have served you so long and served you so well.

When you realize how much effort Life goes to in the use of the Powers of Nature and Forces of the Elements—the plant life spends a whole year's energy to grow you an apple or an orange that you eat in a few moments! That energy and that life and that consciousness is entitled to love and blessings from you.

I wish to develop this within the "I AM" Student Body for many reasons. Its first reaction will be to bless you inside of yourselves. This will also have a very definite effect upon your own digestion, and isn't that comforting? *(applause)* Thank you so much, Precious Ones. Won't you be seated, please; and just remain so.

Now, if in the past you had always called forth the Great Central Sun's Sacred Fire's Purifying Love and Gratitude and Blessing to all the Powers of Nature and Forces of the Elements, instead of imposing discord upon them, it would have been very easy for you to hold your hand out and the Powers of Nature would have given to you their boundless Blessings.

So Beloved Ones, this has many, many Blessings that will come to you once you establish the habit; and once you see how much happiness that habit will bring to you, I am sure you will continue it forever—because you cannot be free, even from the discord within your own flesh or within your affairs or in the atmosphere about you, you cannot be free from limitation and distress until Purification takes place. And the Sacred Fire of Our Love has been called into those Beings that the Great Cosmic Law of Life has created and established to make embodiment

possible in this World and your journey through it—
to use the Powers of Nature and Forces of the Elements to fulfill the Great Divine Plan and reveal your
Mastery.

But remember this: no matter how much Mastery you want in any channel, if you understood that
all Mastery, all Perfection begins with, abides within,
and stays within the Sacred Fire Love from your own
Heart's Flame of the "Mighty I AM Presence," from
the Physical Sun and the Great Central Sun, and
from the Ascended Masters' Great Temples of the
Sacred Fire, and from the Ascended Masters' Heart
Flames of Life, which have given you Their Love
down through the ages—if you will begin to realize
that everything good that you want abides within,
begins manifestation, is sustained by and protected by
the Sacred Fire Love of the Great Central Sun, as
well as your "Beloved Mighty I AM Presence" and
the Ascended Host—this realization must come within
you.

When it does, you will begin to let go of the
habits of the outer self that have been your problems,
your mistakes, your limitations, past and present, because every Activity of the Sacred Fire that you call
forth in outer world conditions to release you from
limitation—They are all the Gift of the Love of some
part of Life! That Sacred Fire Love from the Great

Central Sun is the Master Power of the Universe. It is great enough, and Its Pressure is great enough to hold in Divine Balance and Divine Law and Order, all the Planets of a System around a Sun, and all the Systems of Suns that are held in Perfect Balance around a greater Sun. Until that is understood as the Great Divine Plan of Life, and mankind really understand how much Perfection and Power abide within that Sacred Fire Love, the outer self goes on just in a fragmentary way and does not gain its Freedom, and does not fulfill the Great Divine Plan.

This which I offer for your acceptance is not only the freeing of the Earth from destructive forces, but the first Freedom begins within yourself. The outer self, if it is willing to call forth the Sacred Fire Purifying Love of your own "Blessed Mighty I AM Presence" into every outer physical condition of the Powers of Nature and Forces of the Elements, and give Its Blessing and Purity and Love there, you will find It will repay you infinitely and for Eternity for everything you give.

I shall remind you of This as much as possible until you set the habit; and when you do, you will begin to realize that all the Powers of Nature, all the Blessings that the outer world calls wealth, can come to you as easily as the sunshine can come through your window.

People seek after things in the physical world by the trial and error method and the struggle of the physical self, because they will not let the Sacred Fire Love's Purity and Perfection from the "Mighty I AM Presence" go forth to the rest of Life, and especially to the Powers of Nature and Forces of the Elements. But the individual who understands the Law enough to do this, will have all the proof you want of the Freedom that It brings and the Mastery that becomes yours when you use the Master Power of Love that is the Giver of all. It contains all! The Great Central Sun's Heart Flame, the Heart Flame of your "Beloved Mighty I AM Presence," the Heart Flame of every Ascended Master and Cosmic Being, the Heart Flame of your Physical Sun, those Heart Flames are giving, giving, giving, and expanding, expanding, expanding constantly into outer manifestation all the Perfection that Love is and Love has created and Love manifests.

That Love of which I speak is the Sacred Fire Love that is Eternal, Indestructible Purity and Perfection without limit to produce Manifestation that forever blesses all. And when you begin to call that Sacred Fire Love into everything that you contact in the physical world, you will find Its Sacred Fire Presence not only *purifying* things around you, but you will find It begins to *control* things around you, until the Powers of Nature will be your Friends and bow to you to give you their gifts.

Mankind's selfishness is the prisonhouse of poverty; and if you want freedom from the acceptance of limitation, begin to give that freedom to the Powers of Nature and Forces of the Elements by your Call to your own "Beloved I AM Presence" for Its own Heart's Flame of Purifying Sacred Fire Love to go into every condition that is of the Powers of Nature and Forces of the Elements, and there dissolve and consume the impurity and the discord of mankind's human creation. You not only release the Beings of the Elements and the Powers of Nature from mankind's impurity and discord, but you release at the same time your own flesh bodies from the distress and the limitations that have been created within by discord.

When you are willing to use the Great Cosmic Love of Creation to purify and dissolve and consume everything of imperfection, because you are part of those Powers of Nature, they must of necessity produce that same Purity and Freedom and Blessing within you that you give to the world around you. So you cannot lose, you cannot fail; but you can free yourselves from the limitations that have bound you so long, and have kept from you the Blessings that otherwise you could have without limit—because once you become the Manifestation in the outer self of the continual Calls for the Sacred Fire's Indestructible, Purifying Love to blaze into everything *around* you, It must blaze *in* you because you are a part of the Powers of Nature and Forces of the Elements.

So don't be distressed longer by what mankind has created. Call into yourselves, and call into the world around you Our Sacred Fire's Purifying Love that is limitless; and there is more that We can direct to the whole World than mankind comprehends. When you know how much Sacred Fire Love and Power and Energy and Substance it takes to create a Physical Sun and the Planets of the System, and then to sustain them and keep them in constant motion, but balanced, so Perfection can manifest; when you understand how Great is the Intelligence that directs That, how Great is the Pressure of Energy that holds It in Balanced Action, and you realize that by your love to your "Mighty I AM Presence" and your love to Us, We can draw That into the Powers of Nature around you to control Them, We can draw That within you to control you, and free you from your distress, and free the World from its distress—why longer stay in the chains of mankind's human concepts?

Why not open your mind and ask your "Beloved I AM Presence" and the Ascended Masters to fill your mind with the Ascended Masters' Sacred Fire's Heart Flame of Indestructible, Purifying Love. Fill the mind with Love! Fill your emotional bodies, fill your feeling, fill the flesh of your bodies, fill the atmosphere about you, fill the things that you use with Our Ascended Master Sacred Fire's Indestructible, Purifying Love, and let Us show you what Miracles are! *(applause)* Thank you so much.

You were told long ago that *Miracles are God's Perfection, God's Way of Life uninterfered with by mankind's discord or limitation;* and those Miracles are the "Beloved Mighty I AM Presence" and the Ascended Host's Sacred Fire's Heart Flames of such Love that no human thing can exist within It, and no amount of mankind's discord can ever enter into It and exist longer, because It consumes everything unlike Itself. Within that Consuming there is no discord. Whatever that Sacred Fire Love does, it does harmoniously, and more than that, It is a permanent accomplishment.

If you want Miracles, if you want Perfection, if you want Protection, keep this Command going, and see for yourselves whether I tell you the Truth. I am willing to be proved, but you must use your own consciousness and your own Heart's Flame of your "Mighty I AM Presence'" Sacred Fire's Indestructible, Purifying Love, and call It into yourself. Call It

into the things that bless you. Call It into the things
that other people give you. Call It into the things that
you give other people. Call It into the atmosphere
you breathe. Call It into the Powers of Nature and
Forces of the Elements. And open the Door and let
Us give you the Magnificent Perfection of the Ascended Masters' Octave. It is without limit! It is Invincible and is Eternally Expanding.

There is no such thing as limitation to Us!
There is no lack or limitation in Our Ascended Master Octave, because It is completely the Sacred Fire's
Love, Its Indestructible Purity and Its Power without
limit. We can release that Sacred Fire of Indestructible, Purifying Love with such Pressure, no human
thing on this Earth can move! Do you know what
Pressure it takes to stop all the action of mankind and
the animal creation in this World? Can you comprehend, can you imagine what Pressure of Energy it
takes to shut off the action of all beings on this
World? It has been done, and certain Pressure—at
certain times in the past when mankind wouldn't listen, that Pressure came and shut off the discord; and
It can come again.

But We want to train you, if you care to accept
It, to use the Power as We use It in the Ascended
Masters' Octave, and draw It into the physical condi-
tions to purify them as quickly as possible, and to

hold Perfect Balance wherever you abide, for your convenience, for your Mastery, for your Freedom, and to clothe you with Our Power that enables you to give Help like that to your loved ones and to those of the outer world who know not which way to turn at this time.

Please make the Powers of Nature and Forces of the Elements your Friends; and if you will, you will never have cause to regret it. Destructive activities cannot approach you when you have blest the Powers of Nature and the Forces of the Elements with Our Love, and Its Indestructible Purity that sets them free from distress and limitation.

Oh, use this Power, Beloved Ones! Mankind does not know the use of Energy in the Divine Way of Life. It is without limit! We offer It to you! The outer world can't offer It to you through its discord. What can the outer world's discord give you that is good? Everything good in the Universe depends on the Sacred Fire of Our Love's Indestructible Purity, and *that's why We exist as the Seven Mighty Powers around the Throne! That's why We are called the Seven Mighty Builders,* because We use the Supreme Power that builds only Perfection and gives It to Life to expand more Perfection.

So, if from this hour you will accept Our Love and Our Sacred Fire's Indestructible Purity, as you

will call It into the Powers of Nature and Forces of
the Elements to dissolve and consume everything
mankind's discord has imposed upon the Powers of
Nature, you will know a Freedom and a Happiness
and use of certain Powers you never dreamed you
could use in this embodiment. We are offering This
to you all because of the World's crisis this hour.

May you understand what Love can do for you,
and use It! Use It! Use It everywhere in the physical
octave to do that which nothing else can do; and all
mankind's energy put together cannot do This which
Our Sacred Fire Love's Indestructible Purity can do,
as It produces Perfection in the Powers of Nature and
Forces of the Elements, as It draws forth by Precipitation, out of the atmosphere, the Perfection We want
you to have, the Miracle Way to live Life, and the
Fulfillment of the Divine Plan that not only set you
Free, but sets Free all you contact wherever you pass
by, and you become a steady Blessing, just like the
Sun's Light Rays bless you and the Earth.

Wherever you go, you can be the Illumining
Presence of the Sacred Fire Love's Indestructible Purity that prevents all wrong, everywhere you go the
rest of Eternity. It is worth any effort you make to
gather the Momentum now, enfold yourselves in It,
fill yourselves with It, that It may set you Free; and

then go forward and use It to free others, as We have offered It to free you.

When you understand this Sacred Fire Love is in the Universe, and It is the Controller of all Systems of Worlds, do you not think It can control you? Do you not think It can control your physical affairs? It can control everything mankind does if mankind would use It; and since mankind has used discord to control certain Powers of Nature and Forces of the Elements, there comes the hour when that must stop. So We are asking you to set this habit, that you may be able to stop it in the physical world, as We enfold you in Our Sacred Fire Love's Indestructible Purity that keeps you safe, Indestructible Protection, and Indestructible Release of the things that you need to go forward and fulfill the Great Divine Plan, and reveal what the world calls Miracles.

Blessed Ones, I will not hold you longer, and I hope today I may have illumined to you something of what the Sacred Fire Love of the Seven Mighty Elohim means to Life. Mankind should understand how important It is, when It is placed within the brain structure of every physical body in this World! If mankind would only use Our Hearts' Flame, and the Heart Flame of the "Mighty I AM Presence" of each Life Stream, to pour Its Indestructible Sacred Fire Purity into everything you contact, to purify it and bring all into Divine Order harmoniously and permanently, suffering will cease and limitation will be no more.

We enfold you in Its Healing Presence! It will heal, first of all, those who use It, because if you are willing to heal the World and free mankind, automatically the greater Love from Our Octave wants to heal you and free you from anything that is of limitation.

So go forward and use It without limit; but use It just exactly like you use the air you breathe. Fill yourself with It, and realize that every bit of Perfection depends upon It; and no Perfection has ever been created in this World or any other without It. It's the Supreme Source of everything that is right, and will never create anything that isn't right. So your Security is Eternal, and Purity is Eternal, too, but only comes from the Sacred Fire of Our Love and the Love of your "Mighty I AM Presence." Go forward and use It, use It, use It, and let Us give you the Blessings that will enable you to bless others, until wherever you go the Powers of Nature become purified automatically and become your Protectors, your Suppliers, your Blessings for all time to come.

These things have been placed in this World by the Great Cosmic Law; and the Great Cosmic Law of Manifestation everywhere in interstellar space is the Sacred Fire Love of Indestructible Purity. Use It!

Use It!   Use It, and set all Life free wherever you abide. Send It forth everywhere that discord seems to be; and the more you use It, the more you become It; and the more you use It, the more Invincible you become; and the more you use It, the more you raise into Our Perfection for Eternity!

We clothe you in Our Eternal Sun Presence of Our Hearts' Flames' Indestructible Sacred Fire Love's Indestructible Purity, and complete Mastery over every bit of discord in this World; and We enfold you in all you can ever use the rest of Eternity. Call your "Beloved I AM Presence" into action to make you remember to use It; and then set the rest of Life free wherever you abide. Know what it means to live in the World of the Ascended Masters' Sacred Fire Love's Indestructible Purity and Victory without limit for Eternity, which forever prevents all wrong.

We clothe you in the Victory and Protection of Eternity; and the Peace for which you have called becomes your Reality and your Sun Presence, to forever abide within Its Glory. Thank you with all My Heart.

(Record CD 1487)

Excerpt on Beloved Orion's Flame and Constellation

Beloved Orion

I represent the Threefold Action of Divine Love in the Cosmic Power from the Great Central Sun to this System of Worlds. My Activity comes through the Physical Sun, and from thence I dispense It to those who belong to this System of Worlds. . . .

I wish I might show you an Action of the Fire Element which I am privileged to use, which it is My great Joy to draw forth, and whose Beauty I watch with ceaseless Admiration. My Symbol is a Triangle of three Blue Flames through which play constantly the Pink and the Gold. My Quality, My Authority, My Cosmic Attunement are that of Divine Love, charged with the Cosmic Power from the Great Central Sun which can produce instantly whatever Perfection I choose to call forth.

Just as you would see changeable silk with those three colors, but with the Pink predominant, just so do these Flames continually move. They flood forth the three Qualities which are imperative to draw forth whenever manifestation is to be brought into outer activity.

I work in cooperation with Mighty Cyclopea. Divine Love in the use of the Power of Sight—Pure Divine Love from Our Great Cosmic Activities of

Creation is at all times a building activity. It is an expanding Manifestation of the enjoyment of the Life, Beauty, and the Perfection of Cosmic Action. *Without this Quality of Cosmic Divine Love, you would have no cohesive power in manifestation.* There would be no way and means to hold substance together through which energy could pass, except Divine Love gives of Itself the Qualities that draw all manifestation into harmonious accord. Then only Beauty and Perfection are able to come forth! . . .

. . . You have been told in astronomy there is a Constellation of Orion. That was as much as you ever knew. Yet there is a Focus of Life—a Focus of Light—which stays in Its Divine Pattern in that Constellation through an immeasurable length of time, so far as mankind is concerned. People have not wanted to know much about what was above them. Their attention has been, as your Beloved Saint Germain said, a downward looking; and your World today is a picture of what that produces.

I challenge you, Beloved of the Light, to gaze upon the Constellation which bears My Name! Give It your love and ask for Its Light, Its Intelligence, and Its Love to come back to Earth to free mankind from the shadows. With your Call to Me for the Threefold Power of the Flame of My Cosmic Love, I can assist you and the Earth to more rapidly dissolve the shadows.   *("Voice of the I AM," October 1951)*

CHAPTER XIV
Beloved Elohim Orion

Santa Fe, New Mexico
April 8, 1959

Beloved Ones of the Mighty Saint Germain's Family, Beloved Ones of the Sacred Fire, I wish to bring to your attention tonight not only the necessity to remember the use of your own authority, but I wish to bring to you tonight a clearer Understanding of what tremendous Authority every Life Stream has, to call into this physical octave the Greater Powers and the Greater Manifestations of the Universe around this System of Worlds, and bring into outer action those Master Powers and Manifestations of Life that control everywhere in the Universe about you.

Because of mankind's frightful discord, the feelings have become confused and the mind confused and blinded, so to speak, against the memory that every Life Stream has within the consciousness of the outer self, the Ability, the Power, and the Authority to call into manifestation the Greater Infinite Perfection of the Universe, just the same as the intellect and the feelings have the authority and power to call into manifestation and create that which is discordant.

Now, mankind seems to have no trouble about creating discord. Of course it creates trouble, I grant you that. But in the use of the Faculties and Powers of Life, the outer self has taken the authority to create discord.

I plead with you, with the same fierce determination that destructive forces have used to create evil, I ask you to turn about, and facing your "Beloved I AM Presence" and the Ascended Host, who are willing and ready to assist you, turn back with that same fierce determination, and use your Full Authority and Power to draw into outer conditions, day after day after day, with the Full Power of Control of the Seven Mighty Elohim, the Manifestations that They know are required in physical action to master the hordes of evil.

The Greater Intelligence which has produced the Greater Manifestations in this System of Worlds, knows far beyond the human intellect what Forces are required from the Cosmic Standpoint to master the mass accumulation of mankind's frightful destructive creations. The outer intellect of the individual does not understand how much energy has been used by the sinister force to create evil, but the Ascended Host do. And the Cosmic Beings know well how

long mankind has persistently used the Authority of
Life to use energy destructively in this World. And
therefore, We know what the intellect of man does
not know in the control of the forces that have been
generated in this World. But by your attention and
your Call to your "Beloved I AM Presence" and to
Us, you may know, and you may draw here, and
you may use without limit the Sacred Fire Power
from Our Octave; and unless human beings will understand This and use It and be as aware of Its Presence as they are of their hands and feet, how can It
act for the individual?

The destructive forces have been thoroughly
aware of the results they produce when they use energy destructively. Why cannot the intellect and the
feeling of the people become as aware of Our Presence, as aware of the Sacred Fire, as aware of the
Authority and Power of Life to bring Perfection here
that masters evil!

I want to charge you tonight with the Force and
the Power you have never had, until there stands in
and around you the Full Comprehension and the
wide open flow of the Sacred Fire Power from Our
Octave that you need, My Loved Ones, to hold your
own against the forces that would destroy you.

The destructive forces of mankind's generation
have become so brazen, so completely insane and

fiendish in their destruction, that those who seek the constructive way of Life must be awakened, and they must make some effort themselves to use the Cosmic Law of their own Authority, and to draw into this physical world the Sacred Fire that burns up the evil. And if people will not awaken and will continue to sleep in their acceptance of limitation, then they must go through severe experiences until they do awaken.

But you who have had the Blessing of the Mighty Saint Germain and others of the Ascended Host, in the awareness of your "Mighty I AM Presence," the awareness of Our Action of the Sacred Fire, the awareness of this Greater Intelligence that controls the whole System of Worlds, you can have almost instantly the Release of whatever Sacred Fire you are determined and insistent upon manifesting in this World. And the moment you make up your mind that That is coming here, and you give no quarter to anything else, It will be here! So I offer It! *(applause)* Thank you so much, Precious Ones. Won't you be seated, please; and just remain so.

You take this Command with Me: *"Through the Fiery Authority of my 'Beloved I AM Presence which I AM'!"* You want to give it with Me? *(laughter) "Through the Fiery Authority of the 'Beloved Mighty I AM Presence which I AM' and the Invincible Will of the Ascended Masters' Perfection of Eternal Love, I demand the Master Sacred Fire*

Presence of All-Control of everything in my world! 'I AM' the Sacred Fire Master Presence! 'I AM' the Sacred Fire Master Presence! 'I AM' the Sacred Fire Master Presence that forever prevents anything but Perfection in my world!" Thank you, Precious Ones.

Now you take that Command, you issue That, and release the energy of your Life and the vibration of your words and feelings into the atmosphere about you. Then do you know what happens from the Inner standpoint? Your "Beloved I AM Presence" *immediately* flashes the Sacred Fire into that energy, and then It calls to Us, and We amplify That again, and We can expand That to any degree whatsoever that the condition that you want changed requires.

If I were you, I would, in the secret private Application of your own daily work, acknowledge, *"'I AM' the Master Sacred Fire here that forbids manifestation that is not the Perfection of the Ascended Host!"*

My Dear Ones, if you just take that authority, issue the words and feel that Flame go out, We can move Heaven and Earth to assist you. I hope you feel what I want to bring to you tonight as Courage, as Strength, as Power, and as the Controlling Authority in this World that has the right to bring Ascended Master Perfection here!

Now if you are going to master things in this World, you are going to have to use the word

"Mastery." When you say, *"'I AM' the Sacred Fire Master Control here, and I forbid anything in my world but the Ascended Masters' Perfection that should be here"*–now who of you can tell Me what Ascended Master Perfection should be in your world tonight! Can you tell Me? Well, I know! Why? Because We have already called forth Our Perfection for you by Our Love, because your love has come to Us by your attention upon Us. We have already designed Perfection for you, and This is what I am asking you to draw into the physical octave to make everything easier for you, to make you more aware of the Master Powers of the Sacred Fire that bring you this greater Perfection.

It was your use of the Violet Consuming Flame that has brought you Its Blessings. It is your use of the waters of the Planet that bring you their Blessing. It's your use of electricity that brings you the light. Now if you will use Our Sacred Fire Perfection from Our Octave, which contains Our Divine Plan's Perfection to bless you for Eternity, if you will use It, you will have It. But your authority must be absolutely unyielding when you demand your own Master Sacred Fire Control that comes from the Heart Flame of your "Mighty I AM Presence," or from Its Hand, or from Its Forehead. But the Flame of the Seven Mighty Elohim abiding in your brain structure is the extension of Our Life in you; and therefore,

We have the right to design for you Our Ascended
Master Perfection, if you will use It. *(applause)* Thank
you so much.

This does two things. When you acknowledge
This into yourselves or into your world, you are expanding the Sacred Fire in your own Heart, your
forehead, and you are allowing your "Mighty I AM
Presence" to expand Its Sacred Fire through you.
When you *call the Master Sacred Fire Presence of the Ascended Masters' Divine Plan for you into physical conditions,*
you open the Door from your side of Life, and you
let flow Our Heaven to come into manifestation on
Earth. But, if you take this Stand with absolutely un-
relenting, fierce, determined feeling that that which is
not the Perfection shall not live, and when you are
unyielding to that, you exert your dominion over it,
you open the Door and let Our Sacred Fire Perfection
flood you with the Manifestations from Our Octave,
My Dear Ones, there comes into your outer self, into
your outer experience, those greater Blessings and the
Miracles which must, some day, fill this World.

That helps you to be the builders of the Incoming Civilization that, I assure you, is going to be transcendent beyond words to describe, that will bring
Happiness and Blessings of Peace for Eternity, and
will glorify everything that the Word "God" means.

Now the day you rise up and are determined that everything in your being and world shall be the Ascended Masters' Sacred Fire Mastery over everything else, and shall reveal Perfection here that blesses all forever, it's like ringing a doorbell into Our Octave, and I assure you, We will answer the door.

I just want to charge you tonight with such realization of the Authority and the Power that you have to draw this Perfection of the Sacred Fire from Our Octave into your world, to produce here such manifestations as mankind has never yet beheld but which are to come into this World.

You can live in this in your own individual experiences until such time as the outer world is completely purified. But until then, there is no reason you should not enjoy Our Perfection, because We love you. Our Love has designed Perfection for you. Our Love has given you Part of Our Lives. That Sacred Fire abides within you, and that is your Authority of Mastery over manifestation, whether it be in this World or when you come into Our World. It is Our Authority of the Sacred Fire in your own brain structure, and it is the Authority of your "Blessed I AM Presence" in your own Heart Flame that is given to the outer self to create or bring or to manifest in the physical octave the Perfection of the "Mighty I AM Presence" or the Perfection of Our Octave.

When you give This as much attention as the sinister force gives you—to take away your life and your energy to make it live—when you give Us as much attention as it gives you, we'll always get rid of it. And I think it's time! *(applause)* Thank you so much, Precious Ones.

Now you could have anything and everything in the Universe that is of God, all that is good, when you are determined enough to have it. It all rests within your determination. But *when you just wish for a thing, or just hope it will happen, you don't set up enough magnetic attraction to start the flow of the Sacred Fire by which the thing manifests.* So, I am stimulating tonight your desire and your determination to live in Our World and experience Our Heaven on Earth. And when you take the Stand within yourselves to demand the Mastery and the Manifested Power of Our Love, and you demand It teach the outer self about Us, and just let Love do Its Perfect Work—I assure you there will come such Powers into your outer use, there will come such Manifestations in your experiences as can only bring you Joy. We want you to have that Happiness because that is Our Way of Life. That is the Love We love to give.

So there are two Activities in producing manifestation: *One is to hold the Picture* which is the desire in the feeling world, *to love the Picture,* contemplate it, and love that Mastery over everything. Just love it with everything you are and have, in the contemplation of the Picture and the Call to your "Presence" through love. And *the other is that fierce, positive, determined force within your feeling world that Our Perfection of the Sacred Fire shall come here, and nothing in this World shall prevent it.* And when you say, *"Never shall anything oppose that,"* My Dear Ones, as I speak the Words, surely you feel the Current! *(applause)* Thank you so much, Precious Ones.

When you take your Stand that the evil of mankind's generation shall not be any authority in your world, shall not prevent Heaven on Earth, shall not enslave Life, shall not desecrate what is of God, shall not ruin your Nation, shall not desecrate or destroy mankind, you will release Sacred Fire that consumes the evil. You have the Authority! You have the Power! We are ready to release all the Sacred Fire necessary and forever stop the manifestations of that which produces such distress.

My Dear Ones, in this Great God-given Authority of Life which abides within your Life, it's the same Life as Our Life. It's the Life that has created this System and the Manifestations of Infinity, and that Life uses only the Sacred Fire to produce Manifestation. You are Part of that Life. The Sacred Fire comes from Our Octave into you. You are the

Authority, and you have the right to use It! Therefore, from tonight I hope you will reach up and accept your Mastery. *(applause)* Thank you so much.

The more evil forces threaten to destroy conditions in this World, the more they brag about wiping
out everything, the more you must call for the Sacred
Fire Manifestations that put an end to all evil. There
is no battle from Our Side, and when you take this
fierce, determined Stand, there is no battle in you.
When you say, you *demand the Elohim Mastery Power,
the Elohim Mastery Control, the Elohim Sacred Fire here,*
you leave it with Us as to what to select. We'll always
select the right Activity of the Sacred Fire. We will
always produce the Manifestation that is the next
most important thing that you require, and We will
always release the Power that does away with the
evil.

So, when you exert the Authority of your own
Life Stream, when you design that Pattern of Perfection you want, and with all your Heart, all your feeling you love it, then with all the determination of
your being, you call—you just give no quarter to appearances—you *call your "Beloved I AM Presence" first and
then to Us, for the Elohim Mastery of all in this World to
blaze the Sacred Fire that produces this Perfection.* Then you
do not fight evil, you do not resist evil. There is no
battle. The Flame comes in, and It's all there is!

You know the Sun doesn't battle every morning when it arises, does it? Does it battle the evil on this Planet that mankind has generated? It stays in Its own Realm of Mastery. It pours all Its Blessings to good and evil alike, but if you get hot enough and uncomfortable enough, you will either purify yourselves enough so the Sacred Fire from the Physical Sun is comfortable instead of uncomfortable—and that's all it amounts to.

It sounds easy, doesn't it? And it is! Do you know why? Isn't it much easier to love Perfection from Our Octave and contemplate It filling this World, than it is to contemplate what mankind has already generated and is planning to yet increase destruction. There is no effort in contemplating the Perfection in Our World. All the effort is in the human discord, past and present. And when you rise up and you *issue your Command at night before you go to sleep, and you issue It in the morning when you awaken—there shall not be anything in your being and world but the Seven Mighty Elohim Mastery of the Sacred Fire, and Its boundless Beauty and Perfection is your world for Eternity!*

Give Us the opportunity to bring into your world Blessings you have never yet had, but which will serve you well and will be of great benefit to others, as you hold Them in outer use to fulfill the Great Divine Plan.

So, Blessed Ones, Our Octave is the Master
Presence of the Sacred Fire's Love where only Perfection exists; and therefore, if you are going to master
conditions in this World, if you are going to be Master over them instead of having to live under them,
you are going to have to use that word "Mastery."
But don't in the outer let the human say, "Well, I'm
going to master this thing!" And the first thing the
sinister force says is, "Oh, is that so! Well, now we'll
see who has got the most energy!" And then the battle royal is on.

But when you *call Our Sacred Fire, Our Elohim
Mastery, and Its Sacred Fire Power to control all in this
World,* that's a wholly different thing. Do you know
why? Because the sinister force doesn't want to meet
Us, and We are in that Sacred Fire. That's Our Life!
That's Our Control! That's Our Authority! That's
Our Power! They don't want to meet Us. So if you
want to live in Our World and you want Us to live
with you, We have already abided with you all
through these centuries by the Sevenfold Flame in
your forehead—you have had Part of Our Life within
you.

You've had the Sacred Fire from your
"Presence," the Electronic Body; that Sacred Fire is in
your own Heart. So now if you want the world
around you Our Mastery of the Sacred Fire's Love

and Blessings without limit, you use your authority. You exert your feeling and love for Our Perfection. You issue the Command, and We lower the Fulfillment of your Call into your outer experience and for your use. And you can be clothed in This while the sinister force must pass you by.

I so want to relieve you of your problems, your struggle, and the strain, and the things that are imposed upon you, Precious Ones. If you could see sometimes what comes into your world through radiation alone, just through conditions in which you pass, you would arise with a fierce determination to have your Freedom, from which nothing could turn you aside. So, just be happy children, and come and live with Us, and We will come and live with you.

We have called on you many times, but you didn't hear Us! Do you know why the sinister force gets your attention so many times, and We don't? Because it makes you so uncomfortable in your feeling that you keep the attention on the discomfort. Isn't that so? All right, now you come to Us and you want to be comfortable—then draw the Sacred Fire of Our Love, and you demand Our Elohim Mastery over this World. You demand Our Elohim Mastery over everything in this World blaze Its Sacred Fire Love into you and into everything around you, and you will become so comfortable in That, that you won't want to listen to the sinister force. And the more comfortably you desire to live, the more Power We can exert to flood you with Our Perfection.

So, if We can have your attention upon the Comfort and the Peace and the Love of Our Sacred Fire Mastery, if We can have your attention, We can pour It into you and your world. So, when the discord knocks at your front door, if I were you I would say, "I'm in conference," and you're not available to the destructive forces. I'm quite sure you will profit by the experience.

So, Blessed Ones, just accept Our Love tonight. Oh! We are so willing to give you everything. We so want you free from distress. We want to spend Our Time and Energy flooding your beings and worlds with Perfection that's to be here forever. So come, give Us your attention, and let Us reward you for your willingness to draw into this World that which will bless Life for Eternity.

Go forward, and perhaps when you least expect it, I may prod that determination within you with a feeling, sometime, that will all of a sudden make you arise and exert your Master Sacred Fire Control over this World—which is the allowing of your own "Blessed I AM Presence" through the Unfed Flame in your Heart to release a feeling, a pressure of that Sacred Fire into the atmosphere around you—that not only repels limitation and destruction, but creates and maintains the *advance* in the Fulfillment of the Divine Plan that is already the Divine Plan's completed Action in Our Octave of Life, and which you can draw here when you so determine.

Now many times the intellect says, "Well, how am I going to do all that with all the people in the family and all the people in the business that antagonize me, and they don't believe in the 'I AM' Activity, and they won't do this and they won't do that!" Just leave that with Us. You keep acknowledging your Divine Rights—that means your love to your "Presence" and to Us—and your Mastery by Sacred Fire Power Control of things in and around you. And you charge That forth with the same fierce determination and the same amount of energy that you release when you become—well, when you *have* become in the past—angry about something, for I do not acknowledge that you are going to be angry again in the future! But you know the determination you have turned on when something displeased you and you have just exploded—an awful lot. Oh, that energy, such energy goes forth through those sudden feelings, past and present!

We want the same amount of energy to go forth, but qualified with that Master Presence of the Sacred Fire's Power and Control of things in this

World, until, as you form the habit of This, the momentum begins to build within your Electronic Circle. My Dear Ones, you will come to the time when you can scarcely wish or think for a thing until it comes into manifestation for you, and that is the Divine Way to live Life.

So come with Us, and remember, your determination of the future is Our Love and Sacred Fire's Master Power to flood everything in your world; and when you demand it be flooded, so shall it be established unto you!

But don't waste time looking back. Don't regret anything! What's done is done. It's water over your wheel of Life. Be just concerned with the Heaven We have opened to you with the *accepting* of Our Presence with you, and with your determination to fulfill the Divine Plan that means everything Perfect in your world.

You don't have to draw It from someone else; the "Presence" will automatically provide It for you when you have loved the "Presence" enough. And when you call to Us, We will never fail to answer the Call. Our hearing is perfectly good, and We are not so busy but what We can answer the Call whenever you are determined to have your Mastery manifest Its Perfection in this World.

May the Legions of Our Sacred Fire Love who fulfill Our Commands to Life attend you with Their Boundless Blessings, and the Angelic Host and the Powers of Nature ever be flooding you with Their Blessings, Blessings, Blessings of all the Perfection your Heart can desire until you come into Our Octave forever.

So remember, We are as close to you as you want to be close to Us. And if you use your own authority, and your determination to be free from distress is intense enough, your limitation cannot stay within you another hour longer, because Our Love can take the place of everything that has disturbed you. And then do you know what happens? Then the Words of your Beloved Saint Germain will be fulfilled when He said, "You will say to these disturbing conditions, with a wave of your hand to your adversary you will say, 'Well, is it possible thou didst once disturb me?'" That's the Mastery to which I refer—that Peace, that Power of the Sacred Fire's Love that will have nothing in It and no contact except that which is Peace and Perfection and God made manifest in and around you and for you, with every good thing to bless you forever!

Hold close to Us, if you will; and all together We will wave your hands to the adversary *(laughter)* and be through with contact forever.

Thank you, Precious Ones. And I assure you, We have Legions of Angels so beautiful, so powerful, so loving They can stand beside you and release what brings you only Happiness. They are ready, ready any moment to assist you when you are determined your adversary shall be no more. Thank you.

Let us dispose of the adversary if you exert your authority; and between us, we should make a very comfortable combination and produce circumstances that will glorify you all forever.

Thank you, and with My Love to you all, I bear to you tonight the Love and the Gratitude of the Seven Mighty Elohim because you have remembered Them and you have loved Them; and I assure you, They will remember you and love you in return, far more than you can love Them. From tonight, keep the Door wide open and you shall not want for any good thing.

Thank you with all My Heart.

(Record CD 597)

CLOSING BLESSING
By Beloved Mrs. G. W. Ballard

To the Seven Mighty Elohim, the Seven Mighty Kumaras, the Seven Mighty Chohans, the Seven Great Archangels, we ask Thy Enfolding Radiance to those under this Radiation. Watch Thou between each of us while we are absent one from another. Glorify us quickly with the full Blazing Presence of that Sevenfold Flame of the Seven Mighty Elohim. And Beloved Arcturus, compel the Unfed Flame within to expand and meet the Sevenfold Flame without; and cutting us free from all connection with the discord of the outer world, let us move in the world, but not of it; and pouring into its distress whatever Power of that Cosmic Christ Love from the Great Central Sun is necessary to annihilate all human creation. And that Great Violet Flame covering the Earth in Its Blazing Presence, moves us forward the Authority of Beloved Saint Germain's Freedom, to give It without reservation until all stand Ascended in Thy Octave. And we thank Thee!

INDEX

—B—

balance, 22, 35, 39, 43-5, 56,
93, 95, 101, 141, 167, 272,
276, 280, 283, 286
Bible, 79
Body,
Causal, 32, 153, 160,
183, 253, 255
emotional, 1, 17, 45-6, 49, 53,
69, 73, 112, 134, 166,
186, 189, 192, 200, 208,
221, 229, 274, 284, 288
See also feeling world
physical, 17, 23, 45, 46, 49,
53, 56, 58, 111, 115, 166,
167, 182, 192, 229, 236,
246, 251, 261, 274, 282,
288
brain structure, 1-2, 6-7, 23, 41,
49, 52, 68, 71, 150-2, 156,
162-3, 172, 207, 231, 255,
260-2, 288, 298, 300
Brothers of the Golden Robe,
146-7
business, 53, 136, 194, 200,
211, 217, 221, 257, 308

—C—

Cataclysms, past, 285
Causal Body See Body, Causal
Cave of Symbols, 21
Chicago Class [December
1943], 140

Christ, Cosmic, 12, 13, 28, 37,
67- 70, 72, 77, 78-9, 85, 87,
90, 105, 127, 164, 177, 179-
80, 183, 184-6, 188, 190-1,
194-5, 196, 199, 200-3, 208,
217, 220, 223, 261, 313
civilization, incoming See
New Age
civilizations of the past, 178
colors, ix, 64, 147-8, 205, 209,
244, 291
communism, 223
conferences, world, 215
controversy, 212, 308, 310
cooperation, 45, 46, 54, 93,
224, 261, 291
Cosmic Law, 9, 33, 36, 104,
109, 125-6, 137-8, 142, 158,
176, 184, 210, 215, 221-2,
224, 289, 296
Cosmic Screen, 21, 22, 28, 30,
31
creative activities, 3, 9, 120
See also Inspiration
crossroads of Life's
experiences, 140
crown, 162-3
Cyclopea
Music, on, 63
Orion, with, 291
See also All-Seeing Eye

—D—

Decreeing, 179, 196-7, 240,
293, 296-7
Deliverer come, 242

—V—

veils between, 25, 28
Victory (Quality), 11, 69, 165,
  190-1, 246, 270
Victory, Mighty, 25, 31
Violet Consuming Flame, 8,
  18, 82-3, 88, 94, 125, 160,
  172, 186-8, 191, 200, 212,
  220, 222, 230, 240, 267,
  269-70, 298, 313
Visualizing, 17, 23, 25, 27, 92,
  94, 111-13, 115, 118, 163,
  199, 301
Voice, 197-8

—W—

war, 13, 73, 160, 189, 215, 221
water element, 134, 151
will *See* Free Will
Wisdom, 71, 80, 94, 154
  See also Illumination; Love,
  Wisdom and Power
work, 3, 24, 51, 255, 291, 297,
  301
World, survival of, 260

SERIES